YOUNG KENNEDYS

YOUNG KENNEDYS

THE NEW GENERATION

JAY DAVID ANDREWS

AVON BOOKS  NEW YORK

AVON BOOKS, INC.
1350 Avenue of the Americas
New York, New York 10019

Copyright © 1998 by Bill Adler Books
Front cover photographs by AP/Wide World Photos
Interior design by Kellan Peck
Published by arrangement with Bill Adler Books
Visit our website at **http://www.AvonBooks.com**
ISBN: 0-380-79593-0

Library of Congress Cataloging in Publication Data:
Andrew, Jay David.
   Young Kennedys : the new generation / by Jay David Andrews.
      p.   cm.   Includes bibliographical references (p. 212).
      1. Kennedy family—Biography. 2. Politicans—United States—Biography. 3. Children
of presidents—United States—Biography.
      I. Title.
E843.A53   1998
973.922'092'2—dc21   98-4385
[B]   CIP

First Avon Books Trade Printing: August 1998

AVON TRADEMARK REG. U.S. PAT. OFF. AND IN OTHER COUNTRIES, MARCA REGISTRADA, HECHO
EN U.S.A.

Printed in the U.S.A.

OPM   10 9 8 7 6 5 4 3 2 1

Contents

The Kennedy Family Tree   viii

Introduction   1

*America's Reluctant Royalty . . . and the Princes and Princesses
Now Coming into Their Own*

The Kennedy Family Tree Is Planted   4

*The Nine Children of Rose Fitzgerald & Joseph P. Kennedy and
Their Spouses*

1

THE CHILDREN OF JACQUELINE BOUVIER AND JOHN F. KENNEDY

Caroline Bouvier Kennedy (b. November 27, 1957)   13

Buttons and Walls

John Fitzgerald Kennedy Jr. (b. November 25, 1960)   25

The Whole World's Watching

2

THE CHILDREN OF EUNICE KENNEDY AND ROBERT SARGENT SHRIVER

Robert Sargent Shriver III (b. April 28, 1954)   41

AKA Bobby Cotton

Maria Owings Shriver (b. November 6, 1955)   45
   The Juggler
Timothy Perry Shriver (b. August 29, 1959)   57
   The Priest
Mark Kennedy Shriver (b. February 17, 1964)   61
   The Communitarian
Anthony Paul Kennedy Shriver (b. July 20, 1965)   64
   This Buddy's For You

3
THE CHILDREN OF PATRICIA KENNEDY AND PETER LAWFORD
Christopher Kennedy Lawford (b. March 29, 1955)   73
   The Acting Kennedy
Sydney Maleia Lawford (b. August 25, 1956)   81
   Family Matters
Victoria Francis Lawford (b. November 4, 1958)   86
   Miming Mummy
Robin Elizabeth Lawford (b. July 2, 1961)   89
   The Scientist

4
THE CHILDREN OF ETHEL SKAKEL AND ROBERT F. KENNEDY
Kathleen Hartington Kennedy (b. July 4, 1951)   95
   The Strands That Form Her
Joseph Patrick Kennedy II (b. September 24, 1952)   106
   Wearing His Father's Suits
Robert "Bobby" Francis Kennedy Jr. (b. January 17, 1954) 116
   Keeping the Demons Away
David Anthony Kennedy (b. June 15, 1955–d. April 25, 1984) 124
   The Death of Yellow Dove
Mary Courtney Kennedy (b. September 9, 1956)   134
   A Born Fighter
Michael LeMoyne Kennedy (b. February 27, 1958)   138
   Questions of Judgment
Mary Kerry Kennedy (b. September 8, 1959)   145
   Tsah Wakie Walking the Aisle Alone
Christopher George Kennedy (b. July 4, 1963)   150
   A Chip Off Grandpa Joe
Matthew Maxwell Taylor Kennedy (b. January 11, 1965)   153
   Elliot Ness

Contents

Douglas Harriman Kennedy (b. March 24, 1967)   157
  The Record Breaker
Rory Elizabeth Katherine Kennedy (b. December 12, 1968) 160
  The Trailblazer

5
THE CHILDREN OF JEAN KENNEDY AND STEPHEN SMITH
Stephen Edward Smith Jr. (b. June 28, 1957)   167
  The Kennedy Named Smith
William Kennedy Smith (b. September 4, 1960)   171
  "First Do No Harm"
Amanda Mary Smith (b. April 30, 1967)   182
  Grandpa Joe's Historian
Kym Maria Smith (b. November 29, 1972)   185
  The Irish One

6
THE CHILDREN OF JOAN BENNETT AND EDWARD M. KENNEDY
Kara Anne Kennedy (b. February 27, 1960)   189
  Tested By Tragedy
Edward "Teddy" Moore Kennedy Jr. (b. September 26, 1961) 193
  Smiling Underwater
Patrick Joseph Kennedy (b. July 14, 1967)   203
  In Shadow No More

Recommended for Further Reading   212

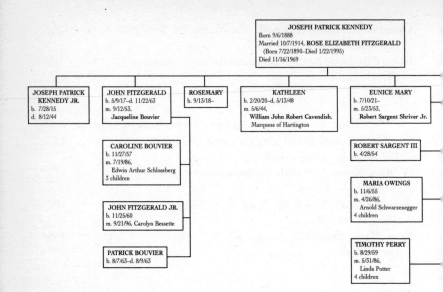

JOSEPH PATRICK KENNEDY
Born 9/6/1888
Married 10/7/1914, **ROSE ELIZABETH FITZGERALD**
(Born 7/22/1890–Died 1/22/1995)
Died 11/16/1969

JOSEPH PATRICK KENNEDY JR.
b. 7/28/15
d. 8/12/44

JOHN FITZGERALD
b. 5/9/17–d. 11/22/63
m. 9/12/53,
Jacqueline Bouvier

ROSEMARY
b. 9/13/18–

KATHLEEN
b. 2/20/20–d. 5/13/48
m. 5/6/44,
William John Robert Cavendish,
Marquess of Hartington

EUNICE MARY
b. 7/10/21–
m. 5/23/53,
Robert Sargent Shriver Jr.

CAROLINE BOUVIER
b. 11/27/57
m. 7/19/86,
Edwin Arthur Schlossberg
3 children

JOHN FITZGERALD JR.
b. 11/25/60
m. 9/21/96, Carolyn Bessette

PATRICK BOUVIER
b. 8/7/63–d. 8/9/63

ROBERT SARGENT III
b. 4/28/54

MARIA OWINGS
b. 11/6/55
m. 4/26/86,
Arnold Schwarzenegger
4 children

TIMOTHY PERRY
b. 8/29/59
m. 5/31/86,
Linda Potter
4 children

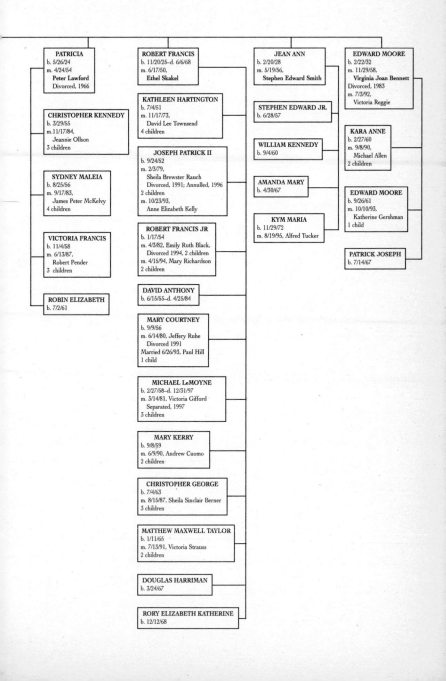

PATRICIA
b. 5/26/24
m. 4/24/54
Peter Lawford
Divorced, 1966

CHRISTOPHER KENNEDY
b. 3/29/55
m.11/17/84,
Jeannie Ollson
3 children

SYDNEY MALEIA
b. 8/25/56
m. 9/17/83,
James Peter McKelvy
4 children

VICTORIA FRANCIS
b. 11/4/58
m. 6/13/87,
Robert Pender
3 children

ROBIN ELIZABETH
b. 7/2/61

ROBERT FRANCIS
b. 11/20/25–d. 6/6/68
m. 6/17/50,
Ethel Skakel

KATHLEEN HARTINGTON
b. 7/4/51
m. 11/17/73,
David Lee Townsend
4 children

JOSEPH PATRICK II
b. 9/24/52
m. 2/3/79,
Sheila Brewster Rauch
Divorced, 1991; Annulled, 1996
2 children
m. 10/23/93,
Anne Elizabeth Kelly

ROBERT FRANCIS JR
b. 1/17/54
m. 4/3/82, Emily Ruth Black,
Divorced 1994, 2 children
m. 4/15/94, Mary Richardson
2 children

DAVID ANTHONY
b. 6/15/55–d. 4/25/84

MARY COURTNEY
b. 9/9/56
m. 6/14/80, Jeffery Ruhe
Divorced 1991
Married 6/26/93, Paul Hill
1 child

MICHAEL LeMOYNE
b. 2/27/58–d. 12/31/97
m. 3/14/81, Victoria Gifford
Separated, 1997
3 children

MARY KERRY
b. 9/8/59
m. 6/9/90, Andrew Cuomo
2 children

CHRISTOPHER GEORGE
b. 7/4/63
m. 8/15/87, Sheila Sinclair Berner
3 children

MATTHEW MAXWELL TAYLOR
b. 1/11/65
m. 7/13/91, Victoria Strauss
2 children

DOUGLAS HARRIMAN
b. 3/24/67

RORY ELIZABETH KATHERINE
b. 12/12/68

JEAN ANN
b. 2/20/28
m. 5/19/56,
Stephen Edward Smith

STEPHEN EDWARD JR.
b. 6/28/57

WILLIAM KENNEDY
b. 9/4/60

AMANDA MARY
b. 4/30/67

KYM MARIA
b. 11/29/72
m. 8/19/95, Alfred Tucker

EDWARD MOORE
b. 2/22/32
m. 11/29/58,
Virginia Joan Bennett
Divorced, 1983
m. 7/3/92,
Victoria Reggie

KARA ANNE
b. 2/27/60
m. 9/8/90,
Michael Allen
2 children

EDWARD MOORE
b. 9/26/61
m. 10/10/93,
Katherine Gershman
1 child

PATRICK JOSEPH
b. 7/14/67

Introduction

America's Reluctant Royalty . . .
and the Princes and Princesses
Now Coming into Their Own

How fascinated are Americans with the Kennedys?

Here is one illustrative answer: In March 1997, the New York *Daily News* and the *New York Post* each ran photos of Caroline Kennedy Schlossberg *walking her dog*.

These were two different pictures taken by two different photographers, and the only thing newsworthy about the woman performing this most mundane of human activities was that it was JFK's daughter (or, as some would describe her, JFK Jr.'s sister!) doing the walking.

But *why* is America so fascinated with the Kennedys? Perhaps because they embody both the best and the worst that a large and famous family can be?

Throughout the last couple of decades, the Kennedys have embraced noble causes while at the same time involved themselves in scandals involving alcoholism, drug abuse, adulterous affairs, and all other manner of sordid scenarios.

A popular perception of the *male* branch of the Kennedy family can best be illustrated by, of all things, a joke from one of Conan O'Brien's late-night TV monologues.

According to Conan, *USA Today* ran a quiz that would tell you if you were a sex addict. The criteria were: 1) needing sex all the time; 2) thinking about sex all the time; and 3) if your last name rhymed with "Shmennedy."

Ouch.

Aside from the scandals, though, even the most passionate of Kennedy haters would admit that the family is responsible for a phenomenal amount of philanthropic work, including the Peace Corps, the Special Olympics, Very Special Arts, the Joseph P. Kennedy Jr. Foundation, the Kennedy Center for the Performing Arts, and other cultural and social organizations that do a great deal of good.

What is so remarkable about the Kennedy family is how often both the finest and basest tendencies of the family manifest themselves in the same person.

Michael Kennedy worked diligently to help the poor afford home heating oil, but admitted to alcoholism when he was accused of having an illicit affair with a fourteen-year-old babysitter.

Bobby Kennedy Jr. is an environmental activist who was once addicted to heroin.

Joe Kennedy II is a Democratic politician who is a staunch advocate of social issues, and yet was accused of verbally abusing his ex-wife during their marriage.

William Kennedy Smith is a doctor dedicated to helping the sick, but he was accused of rape and later arrested in a bar brawl.

Somehow, it seems, saints and sinners abound not only in the Kennedy family as a whole but in the public and private actions of each of its members.

This duality is what keeps the Kennedys in the newspapers and makes all their accomplishments—as well as all their peccadilloes—news.

Young Kennedys: The New Generation looks at the twenty-nine members of the third generation of this august family.

In the twenty-one-year period from 1951 through 1972, six of Rose and Joe Kennedy's nine children gave the world a total of twenty-nine third-generation Kennedys.

In 1951, Bobby and Ethel's daughter Kathleen was Rose and Joe's first grandchild; in 1972, Jean and Stephen Smith's adopted daughter was their twenty-ninth.

Today, several of these third-tier Kennedys are so well known they are "first-name" only celebrities: Caroline, Maria, John, Bobby, Ted, and, of course, Willie.

We will begin our visit with a look at the six children of Joe and Rose who started it all.

The Kennedy Family Tree
Is Planted

The Nine Children of Rose Fitzgerald & Joseph P. Kennedy
and Their Spouses

Joseph Patrick Kennedy wed Rose Fitzgerald Kennedy in 1914. They had nine children. This section provides brief biographical profiles of this *second* generation of Kennedys, with details on their lives, careers, and marriages. The children are profiled in chronological order, from the oldest of Joe and Rose's kids, Joe Jr., to their youngest, Ted.

JOSEPH P. KENNEDY JR. (1915–1944)

Lieutenant Joseph P. Kennedy, Joe and Rose's firstborn child, lived a brief but valorous life. He died at the age of twenty-nine when his plane exploded over the English Channel on August 12, 1944, after only twenty minutes in the air.

Joe had volunteered to fly a top-secret mission designed to wipe out a cache of unmanned Nazi V-1 rockets, terrible weapons that the Germans had been using to rain devastation on Great Britain.

Joe's mission was to take off in a gutted plane (nicknamed *Zootsuit Black*) that was filled with an enormous amount of explosives, put it on autopilot while aimed at the missile stronghold, and then parachute to safety with his copilot. The plane exploded prematurely, however, and Joe and his copilot were killed instantly. (Military historians today tend to lean toward an electronic malfunction as the cause of the explosion.) Two priests were sent to Hyannis Port, Massachusetts, the Kennedy home, to give the bad news to Rose and Joe.

Jack Kennedy ultimately compiled a collection of tributes to his big brother titled *As We Remember Joe* (1944) as a Christmas gift to his parents. JFK wrote the introduction to the volume, eloquently writing of his brother, "His worldly success was so assured and inevitable that his death seems to have cut into the natural order of things."

Joe Jr. never married.

JOHN FITZGERALD KENNEDY (JFK) (1917–1963)

The thirty-fifth president of the United States, Jack was born in Brookline, Massachusetts, on Tuesday, May 29, 1917, the first president born in the twentieth century. He was named after his maternal grandfather, John F. "Honey Fitz" Fitzgerald.

He was assassinated, apparently by Lee Harvey Oswald, in Dallas, Texas, on Friday, November 22, 1963. Assassination conspiracy theorists continue to suggest that Oswald did not act alone, although the United States government has never acknowledged that there was another shooter.

JFK served in World War II from September 1941 through April 1945. He was the skipper of a patrol torpedo boat, the *PT–109*, and won a Purple Heart for saving an injured crewman after his ship was sunk. After his discharge from the navy, he worked as a journalist, was a U.S. Representative from 1947–1953, and a Senator from 1953–1961.

He was elected president on November 8, 1960, defeating

Republican Richard Nixon with 49.7% of the popular vote. Highlights of his administration include the Bay of Pigs Invasion in 1961; the establishment of the Peace Corps in 1961; involvement in the Civil Rights issue; the August 1961 Berlin Crisis; the 1962 Cuban Missile Crisis; the July 1963 Nuclear Test Ban Treaty; the staunch commitment to putting a man on the moon; and the 1961 ratification of the Twenty-third Amendment to the Constitution.

JFK was the author of several books, including *When England Slept* (1940), *Profiles in Courage* (1961), and *A Nation of Immigrants* (1964).

Jack married Jacqueline Bouvier (1929–1994) in 1953. They had three children, though son Patrick died shortly after birth. Jackie, known to this day as the most fashionable First Lady ever, remodeled the White House and took TV viewers on a televised tour of the great house in February 1962. She was riding in the limousine with her husband when he was mortally wounded. In 1968, Jackie remarried, to Greek millionaire Aristotle Onassis. In 1975, she became a book editor at Doubleday. She died in May 1994. Sotheby's conducted an auction of her belongings in April 1996 that generated over thirty million dollars for her children.

ROSEMARY KENNEDY (1918–)

Rosemary Kennedy, originally named "Rose Marie", was Joe and Rose's first daughter. She was born mildly retarded (an IQ below 100) reportedly because the nurse assisting in her delivery was instructed to delay the birth until the doctor arrived (as was the prevailing custom of the time). The nurse did as she was told and deliberately prevented Rosemary's head from leaving the birth canal, thereby depriving her brain of oxygen.

Rosemary's parents made every effort to help her by hiring private tutors and special nurses, but to no avail. As Rosemary grew into her teens and twenties, she began having mood swings that often turned violent.

When Rosemary was twenty-three, her father Joe consented to a new and experimental operation that the doctors told him might help her achieve a more normal level of intelligence.

This surgery—a prefrontal lobotomy—had disastrous results. Her nephew Anthony Shriver has said that the surgery made her go from being mildly retarded to being severely retarded.

Eunice Kennedy Shriver went public with her sister's retardation in a September 1961 article in *The Saturday Evening Post* in which she wrote, "Early in life Rosemary was different. She was slower to crawl, slower to walk and speak than her two bright brothers. My mother was told she would catch up later, but she never did. Rosemary was mentally retarded."

Rosemary's mother Rose, who reportedly was not told of the surgery until 1961, later wrote of the operation: "The operation eliminated the violence and the convulsive seizures, but it also had the effect of leaving Rosemary permanently incapacitated. She lost everything that had been gained during the years by her own gallant efforts and our loving efforts for her. She had no possibility of ever again being able to function in a viable way in the world at large."

Today, Rosemary lives quietly at St. Coletta's Convent in Wisconsin, where she receives compassionate, round-the-clock care. Rosemary has resided at St. Coletta's for decades, and many members of the Kennedy family visit her regularly. She is especially close with her nephew Anthony and her niece Caroline Kennedy Schlossberg.

Rosemary never married.

KATHLEEN "KICK" KENNEDY (1920–1948)

Kathleen Kennedy, Rose and Joe's second daughter, was beautiful, smart, and—true to her nickname—a real "kick" to be around.

After her husband, the British Marquess of Hartington,

was killed during World War II, she fell in love with Lord Peter Fitzwilliam, a Protestant, who was married at the time. Rose and Joe were adamantly against their romance but, in 1948, Joe Sr. reluctantly agreed to meet Fitzwilliam.

Before the meeting, Kick and Peter decided to spend a couple of days relaxing in Cannes. The day they were scheduled to leave Paris for Cannes, violent thunderstorms were predicted for the area. Against the warnings of the pilot, Fitzwilliam ordered an eight-seat plane into the air. The plane ended up flying straight into terrible winds and rain, and the pilot was blown off course.

The plane tragically crashed into a mountain in the Rhône valley, killing all four aboard. Joe Sr., who was in Europe at the time, flew to the site of the crash and insisted on seeing his daughter's mangled and burnt body. Kathleen, who was twenty-eight at the time of her death, was buried in England in her late husband's family plot. Rose Kennedy did not attend the funeral.

Kathleen married William J. Cavendish, the Marquess of Hartington, in 1944 at the age of twenty-four. Cavendish was killed in France during World War II by a German sniper's bullet in September 1944, making Kick a widow after less than six months of marriage. They had no children.

EUNICE MARY KENNEDY (1921–)

Eunice Kennedy, Rose and Joe's third daughter and fifth child, is best known for being the founder of the pioneering organization, the Special Olympics, a worldwide group that involves the mentally retarded in sports training and competition.

She is also the executive vice president of the Joseph P. Kennedy Jr. Foundation, the organization founded by her father and named after her brother Joe Jr., who was killed during World War I.

Eunice graduated from Stanford University with a BS in

Sociology and is the recipient of many honorary degrees for her groundbreaking work on behalf of the mentally retarded.

Eunice married R. Sargent Shriver Jr. (1915–) in 1953. They had five children. Shriver ran for vice president in 1972 and president in 1976.

PATRICIA KENNEDY (1924–)

Pat Kennedy, probably best known for having married the actor Peter Lawford, has been involved in many charitable pursuits throughout her life. She also was a staunch supporter of her brother Jack's political career and agreed to postpone her divorce from Lawford until after Jack's 1964 election.

Pat is known to have abused alcohol and drugs during her married years, perhaps due to Peter Lawford's notorious womanizing and his own substance abuse problems.

In recent years, Pat has been a champion of her son Chris' acting career, while continuing to devote time to her charitable interests and, of course, to being a grandmother.

Pat married actor Peter Lawford (1923–1984) in 1954; they divorced in 1965, after JFK's assassination. They had four children. Pat never remarried.

ROBERT "BOBBY" FRANCIS KENNEDY (RFK)
(1925–1968)

Bobby Kennedy was his brother Jack's campaign manager and later served as President Kennedy's attorney general from 1961–1964. During his tenure as attorney general, Bobby promoted the Civil Rights Act of 1964 and also pursued a racket-busting policy that created enormous animosity between the Kennedys and organized crime factions. After JFK's assassination, President Johnson chose Hubert Humphrey as his vice-presidential running mate instead of Bobby. RFK then resigned and was elected a senator for New York state. At a campaign stop in California during his 1968 campaign for the

Democratic presidential nomination, Bobby was assassinated by Jordanian radical Sirhan Sirhan.

Bobby married Ethel Skakel (1928–) in 1950. They had eleven children.

JEAN ANN KENNEDY (1928–)

Jean Kennedy was awarded the ambassadorship to Ireland in 1992 by President Bill Clinton. Jean has also stewarded the Kennedy family's Very Special Arts program and has worked the political campaigns for several of the politicians in the family.

Jean married Stephen Smith (1927–1990) in 1956. They had two children and adopted two children.

EDWARD "TED" MOORE KENNEDY (1932–)

Senator Ted Kennedy is the youngest Kennedy child, and has had to carry on the Kennedy legacy as the only surviving male of the family. He has been embroiled in scandal throughout his life, most notably the Chappaquiddick incident in which Mary Jo Kopechne drowned. In recent years, he seems to have conquered his drinking and drug problem and appears to be very happily married in his second marriage. Criticisms of his personal life aside, he is highly regarded—even by his enemies—for his tireless work as a U.S. senator.

Ted married Joan Bennett (1936–) in 1958. They had three children. They divorced in 1981. Ted married attorney Victoria Reggie (1954–) in 1992. She has two children from a previous marriage.

THE CHILDREN OF
JACQUELINE BOUVIER
AND JOHN F. KENNEDY

Caroline Bouvier Kennedy

(b. November 27, 1957)

BUTTONS AND WALLS

I know why it's important to protect your privacy.
—CAROLINE KENNEDY SCHLOSSBERG

JFK'S daughter Caroline—the little girl her daddy called "Buttons"—was the first person to confirm to John F. Kennedy that he had, indeed, been elected president of the United States.

She did so on the bright November morning after the 1960 election by leaping onto JFK's sleeping form with all the weight of her tiny, three-year-old body, rough-housing him awake, and then saying, "Good morning, Mr. President!" He had fallen asleep before the previous night's final poll results were in, but the children's nanny, Maud Shaw, correctly deduced he had won the presidency when she saw a Secret Service agent standing on the lawn of Kennedy's home early the next morning. Shaw then told Caroline what to say after she had awakened her father.

Ever since that auspicious autumn morning, Caroline Bouvier Kennedy Schlossberg's identity has been to some extent

13

defined by the memory of her slain father and, in the late eighties and nineties, by the presence of her photogenic brother John Jr., the anointed and, many believe, inevitable heir to Camelot—perhaps also the White House. Regardless of her many accomplishments throughout her life—her myriad roles as lawyer, writer, philanthropist, and mother—Caroline cannot escape the association of being JFK's daughter and JFK Jr.'s sister, not to mention the worldwide notoriety of being Jackie's daughter.

Thus, this inevitable question: Was Caroline Kennedy making a personal statement by titling her second book, *The Right to Privacy*?

Caroline, often perceived as the most private of the Kennedy third generation, has deliberately avoided the press for the majority of her life. Perhaps it should instead be said that she has deliberately *controlled* the media's access to her with an iron will and an unwavering sense of authority. While promoting *The Right to Privacy* in 1995, Caroline agreed to be interviewed only in her publisher's offices (reporters weren't getting anywhere *near* her Park Avenue co-op apartment) and journalists were all informed of "taboo" topics and questions, too-sensitive subject areas that included her mother's nemesis, persistent *paparazzo* Ron Galella, and her father's assassination. As another condition for the interview, Caroline also refused to be interviewed or photographed without her coauthor.

Journalist Patricia Morrisroe, writing in a November 1995 *Vogue* profile of Caroline and her *Right to Privacy* co-author Ellen Alderman, noted that "Being a friend of Caroline's means never talking to the press. Betrayal of that understanding results in automatic banishment."

It seems as though Caroline Kennedy has determinedly spent much of her life building walls around herself and her family, and yet despite all that, she is a beloved figure who still exudes the Kennedy aura whenever she appears in public.

The media and Kennedy watchers around the world still clamor for details about her most private of private lives.

Caroline Kennedy was born on Wednesday, November 27, 1957, at New York's Lying-in Hospital at the Cornell University Medical Center. She was delivered by Cesarean section; weighed seven pounds, two ounces; and her father described her as being "as robust as a sumo wrestler." When Caroline was three weeks old, she was baptized by Cardinal Richard Cushing at St. Patrick's Cathedral in New York City. When Caroline was two years old, she spoke her first words, and since she *was* the daughter of a perpetually traveling politician, they were "plane," "good-bye," "New Hampshire," "Wisconsin," and "West Virginia." When Caroline turned three, her daddy was the new president-elect of the United States.

Caroline's early years in the White House were like a fairy tale of which she has admitted she has little genuine recollection. Her room was decorated all in pink, and after her brother John was born, Caroline used to delight in interpreting his baby talk for her father. Even though Jackie frowned on exploiting her children for public relations purposes, JFK would willingly allow the press to photograph Caroline and John. He also allowed the children to visit him in the Oval Office, even when he was in the midst of a meeting with some political bigwig or foreign dignitary. It is apparent that JFK intuitively realized that even though he was the most powerful man in the world (and thus could easily intimidate other world leaders), the presence of children in his life humanized him and helped anxious White House visitors relax. Once, during one of JFK's frequent press conferences, Caroline teetered unannounced into the room in a nightgown and high heels. JFK continued on as though this was the most normal occurrence in the world, and in a way, it was.

He was a father first, and he never let the country—or the world—forget it.

JFK insisted that his children be brought to him in the Oval Office each morning before his day began, and he would spend some time playing with them before tackling his duties. Caroline would dance for her daddy while little John crawled around under his father's desk.

Sometimes JFK's willingness to allow access to his children backfired on the president. Once, when a reporter asked little Caroline (who was four or five at the time) what her father was doing, she told him that her daddy was upstairs with his shoes and socks off. "He's not doing anything," she bluntly revealed in the forthright manner of small children everywhere.

Caroline rode horses when she was five, and made mud pies with her friends on the grounds of the White House.

Caroline was America's princess and in the halcyon years before Dallas, it seemed as though she would grow up happy, unspoiled, and privileged, with loving parents watching over her and guiding her way. Then the calendar turned to Friday, November 22, 1963, the most horrible Friday in Caroline Kennedy's life.

Caroline was told of her father's death by her nanny, Maud Shaw. Nanny Shaw wrote in her book, *White House Nannie*, that telling Caroline that her father had died was one of the most dreadful tasks she'd ever had to live through. When Shaw told the little girl that her father was in heaven with her brother Patrick, Caroline cried so intensely, she began gasping for air and Shaw feared she might choke. Shaw comforted her, but losing her father was a severe and tragic emotional injury to Caroline's psyche, and perhaps the single most pivotal moment in her life.

On their last day in the White House, Caroline and John, whose birthdays are November 27 and November 25, respectively, shared a joint birthday party, complete with party hats and ice cream. Jackie, who had recently had to stoically watch her tiny son salute his father's coffin on his third birthday, was adamant that life go on for her children in as normal a manner as possible.

But Caroline was feeling anything but normal. Caroline's childhood French teacher, Jacqueline Hirsh, in an oral history archived at the John F. Kennedy Memorial Library, recalled, "She just looked ghastly. She was so pale and her concentration broken." Hirsh also put to rest the question as to how much of what had happened Caroline understood. "She comprehended the assassination, fully, absolutely. You could see it was on her mind, that it was rough on her. But she never did complain, never."

Caroline withdrew emotionally for a time, shunning the press and others wanting her attention, and hiding when reporters were around. After a brief period living in Washington, Jackie decided that they all needed to get away from the White House environs and the D.C. press. In September of 1964, Jackie and the two children moved into the Carlyle Hotel in New York City while the fifteen-room, Fifth Avenue apartment she had purchased for $200,000 (and would eventually spend an additional $125,000 redecorating) was being readied.

As soon as they had relocated to New York, Jackie enrolled Caroline in the Convent of the Sacred Heart and walked her to school every morning. Caroline dutifully wore the Sacred Heart uniform—red leotard, gray flannel jumper, white blouse, and gray blazer—and the teachers and the parents of the other children all tried to treat Caroline as normally as possible. Some parents went so far as to deliberately not invite Caroline to their children's birthday parties for fear of looking as though they were trying to win favor.

Jackie's marriage to Aristotle Onassis in October of 1968 was apparently upsetting to Caroline. Reports described her as looking "glum," "dazzled," and "wan" at the ceremony, but over time, she seemed to develop a real affection for Onassis. It took her a year to stop addressing him as "Mr. Onassis," but amazingly, she eventually ended up actually calling him "Daddy." In *Prince Charming*, the story is told of the time Jackie went to Aristotle and told him that Caroline had a particular affection for a certain horse. Onassis cut her off and ordered her to immediately buy the horse, its mother, its sisters, and its brothers for Caroline. After Onassis's death, Caroline reportedly told then-boyfriend Juan Cameron, "I didn't see him that much, but I really did love him."

In 1969, Caroline transferred to the exclusive Brearley School for three years and then, in 1972, entered Concord Academy in Massachusetts as a sophomore. She showed up for school with her mother and five Secret Service agents. Caroline's Secret Service protection expired when she turned sixteen the following winter, and Jackie hired two full-time private guards to protect Caroline from then on. During the summer of her first year at Concord, Caroline campaigned for both John Kerry and presidential candidate George McGovern. She also played first string defense for Concord's girls' lacrosse team.

In 1973, Caroline spent six weeks in Tennessee working on a documentary about Appalachian miners. She lodged with a miner's family and asked for no special treatment or consideration. "You would never know she's the daughter of the late president and so rich," a native told the Knoxville *News-Sentinel*. "She goes up and down these mountains just like us other hillbillies!"

In February and March of 1975, during her senior year at Concord, Caroline participated in a six-week off-campus project that involved a 26,000-mile trip through Beirut, Khartoum, and Cairo for television. Caroline worked as an unpaid intern on the film that eventually was aired on the NBC magazine show, *Weekend*. One of the crew members was later

quoted as remarking that Caroline "just picks up on people—
on who's real and who's phony."

Caroline graduated with honors from Concord Academy
in June 1975 and decided to spend a year in London studying
art at Sotheby's. She had refused to "come out" at a debutante
ball and also broke tradition by not immediately entering college after graduation. It was in October of 1975, during Caroline's stay at family friend Sir Hugh Fraser's home in London,
that a bomb exploded in Fraser's red Jaguar. It had been
parked on the street outside his home; the bomb killed a by-
stander and terrified Jackie, who insisted that Caroline return
home immediately. If Fraser had not received a phone call
minutes before the bomb went off, he and Caroline would
have been in the car when it exploded and both would have
been killed instantly.

Caroline refused to return to the United States, however,
instead remaining in London to complete the balance of the
Sotheby's program.

In September 1976, Caroline enrolled at Radcliffe, the
women's counterpart to Harvard University. Harvard was the
alma mater of her father, as well as her uncles, Bobby and
Ted. Her cousin Kathleen Kennedy had also attended Radcliffe. While attending college, Caroline lived in the Winthrop
House (known on campus as "Kennedy House"), the house
where all the members of her family had lived when they were
in school. Caroline's cousins Steven Smith Jr., and David and
Robert Kennedy Jr., were attending Harvard at the same
time that Caroline was at Radcliffe, and during these years,
Caroline was especially close with her troubled cousin David.
(See the chapter on David Kennedy for details on Caroline
and cousin Sydney Lawford's involvement in the events surrounding David's overdose death.) Caroline's brother John
was attending nearby Phillips Academy at this time.

Caroline drove a BMW while at Radcliffe and was known
as a witty raconteur with a wonderful sense of humor. She

was also known as someone who could understandably be detached and closed off when she wanted to be. She also had the reputation of being a lousy tipper at restaurants.

In May 1977, Caroline applied for and was given a job as a copy person for the New York *Daily News*. She earned $156.89 a week and her duties included fetching coffee for the paper's editors, many of whom asked for the java just so they could say Caroline Kennedy got them coffee!

Even though she tried to keep a low profile, her fame and reputation followed her like an enormous shadow. She was particularly embarrassed one day when wire service photos of her eating lunch were sent to the *Daily News* and arrived there before she had even returned to work.

While working for the *Daily News*, Caroline was sent to Elvis Presley's Graceland mansion in Memphis, Tennessee, in August 1977 to cover Presley's funeral for the paper. Presumably unhappy with the tone of the final piece, the *Daily News* rejected Caroline's story. She immediately sold it to *Rolling Stone*, and in the September 22, 1977 issue of the magazine, the article, "Graceland," with Caroline Kennedy's byline, was published. Caroline's writing in the article, while perhaps a bit spiritless, was nonetheless tight and evocative.

In April 1977, Caroline appeared at an antiapartheid rally at Radcliffe, and in the winter of that year, she traveled to China for an extended visit with several cousins, aunts, and her uncle Ted.

In January 1978, while Caroline was in China, a warrant was issued for her arrest for failure to appear in court to answer a speeding summons. On the day after this story appeared in *The New York Times*, Jackie sent three of her lawyers to court on Caroline's behalf and the arrest warrant was withdrawn. The judge in the case was quoted as saying, "For a $25 fine, she brings in $3,000 worth of attorneys."

In September 1978, Caroline, attempting to pursue her interest in writing and journalism, applied for a job as a feature writer for the Los Angeles *Herald-Examiner*. She got the job, but had to decline acceptance because the press would not leave her alone and it was obvious there was no way she would be able to do her job without becoming part of the stories herself.

During her junior year at Radcliffe, Caroline dated Tom Carney, an aspiring screenwriter who used to work at Doubleday. Her mother introduced them and even tried to help Carney get one of his scripts produced through her connections, but to no avail. Carney reportedly broke up with Caroline because he couldn't stand the constant media attention and did not want to end up being known as "Mr. Caroline Kennedy."

In 1980, Caroline graduated from Radcliffe and moved into a $2,000 a month, three-bedroom triplex apartment on the upper West Side of Manhattan with three roommates—two male friends and a girlfriend. Caroline's share of the rent was $500 a month, and she began working in the Film and Television Development Office of the Metropolitan Museum of Art.

The Kennedy name, of course, followed Caroline, and attracted all types of attention. In 1981, a deranged thirty-five-year-old California lawyer began stalking and harassing Caroline, going so far as to attempt to break into her apartment building. He ended up spending a year in jail. In 1984, a former mental patient threatened to blow up the Metropolitan Museum of Art and kill Caroline. He, too, was ultimately incarcerated.

During these years, Caroline had her share of dates, including photographer Peter Beard, who taught her how to use a camera, fashion designer Willie Woo, *Rolling Stone* publisher Jann Wenner, and *Daily News* reporter Rick Licato.

But it was in late 1981, at a dinner party, that Caroline met the man who would ultimately become her husband: multimedia designer and writer Edwin Schlossberg, a man thirteen years older than she, and someone who was independent and self-confident enough to be not the least impressed with her family.

Caroline and Ed's relationship deepened over time and they were married on Saturday, July 19, 1986, a day that, unfortunately, was the seventeenth anniversary of her uncle Ted's accident at Chappaquiddick. Caroline was twenty-eight; Ed was forty-one. They were married at Our Lady of Victory Church in Hyannis Port, Massachusetts, at the family "compound." There were 425 guests at the wedding: twenty-one were Ed's, the other 404 were guests of the Kennedy family.

Even though the couple's wedding was in Hyannis Port, far enough away from Manhattan, Boston, and Washington to hopefully guarantee some semblance of privacy, the press attention surrounding the wedding was so overwhelming that the Kennedy family actually had to have air traffic over the family compound banned during the hours of the wedding and the reception that followed.

Caroline's brother John was Ed's best man, and her cousin Maria Shriver was her maid of honor. Because Ed was Jewish there was no Catholic mass, but also no rabbi. Caroline's grandmother Rose watched part of the ceremony from a wheelchair on the porch of the Kennedy house, and Carly Simon sang at the reception. George Plimpton provided a fireworks display afterwards, and the couple spent a month in Hawaii and Japan on their honeymoon. The newlyweds bought a New York co-op near Jackie upon their return, but after Caroline got pregnant, they moved into a $2.65 million, twelve-room apartment on Park Avenue. Ed decorated the apartment while Caroline tended to her law school studies. She had entered law school in 1985 and continued her studies throughout her courtship and marriage.

Caroline graduated a Stone Scholar in the top ten percent of her graduating class from Columbia Law School in June 1988, and shortly thereafter, on June 24, went into labor with their first child.

Rose Schlossberg was born on June 25, 1988 at 3:30 A.M., weighing seven pounds twelve ounces, at New York Hospital's Cornell Medical Center where Caroline had registered as "Mrs. Sylva." Caroline and Ed's second child, Tatiana, was born two years later on May 5, 1990, and their third child, a boy they named John, was born on January 19, 1993.

Caroline passed the bar exam in February 1989, the first time she attempted it. Caroline's proficiency at the bar was another factor adding to her brother John's embarrassment at needing three tries to pass it. The press wouldn't let up on reminding the world that Caroline had only needed one try! (See the chapter on John F. Kennedy Jr.)

It was around the time that Caroline began working on writing her first book, *In Our Defense: The Bill of Rights in Action*. She cowrote it with a friend she had met in law school, Ellen Alderman. *In Our Defense* was published in 1991 and was a bestseller. Caroline and Ellen Alderman published their second book, *The Right to Privacy*, in 1995.

In recent years, Caroline has been on the board of trustees of the John F. Kennedy Memorial Library and has actively participated in the administration of the library's museum section. Dave Powers, a former aide of her father, said of Caroline, "She has never missed a meeting. She contributes ideas all the time on how to make the museum more appealing to the new generation who never lived through the Kennedy years." She is also very involved in the annual Profiles in Courage Award, named after her father's Pulitzer Prize-winning book. She is also the honorary chairman of the American Ballet Theatre.

Caroline and Ed spend many weekends at their country home, an enormous converted barn in the Berkshires of Massachusetts. Her *Right to Privacy* editor Peter Gethers has described Caroline as "astonishingly well-adjusted to her fame," and notes that "she is remarkably poised and self-effacing when in a public situation." A journalist interviewing Caroline for *Vogue* magazine noted that Caroline drank her coffee black rather than call attention to the fact that she had asked for it with cream.

Caroline Kennedy, the only daughter of John and Jacqueline Kennedy, has obviously come to terms with her fame, as well as her name. She no longer tries to rudely cut ahead of people in line, as she once did in an ice cream parlor when she was younger, admonishing everyone that she was Caroline Kennedy. Nor does she neglect her appearance the way she did before she met Edwin Schlossberg.

Caroline Kennedy in her fourth decade is elegant, refined, intelligent, dignified, warm, and socially conscious.

In a sense, Caroline Kennedy, the young lady known to her father as "Buttons," has now unquestionably become her mother's daughter.

John Fitzgerald Kennedy Jr.
(b. November 25, 1960)

THE WHOLE WORLD'S WATCHING

I think [Caroline and I] have a strong sense of my father's legacy and how important it is and we both respect it enormously. But at the same time, there is a sense of—a realization that things are different and that he would have wanted us to go on our own lives and not reenact his. . . . You have to remember that both my sister and I, particularly myself, view my father's administration through the color of others and the perceptions of others and through photographs and through what we have read. And so it's difficult for us to discern much about him independently of what other people's impressions are.
—JOHN JR., May 1992

If your father was a doctor, and your uncle are doctors, and all your cousins are doctors, and all the family ever talks about is medicine, there's a good chance maybe you're going to be a doctor too. But maybe you want to be a baker.
—JOHN JR., August 1993

John F. Kennedy Jr.'s *George* magazine business card reads simply, "John Kennedy."

What should we make of that?

What should we read into the fact that John does not feel the need to include the "F" for "Fitzgerald," or, more significantly, the "Jr.," which would acknowledge just who his father was and that he is, indeed, his father's son?

Is John F. Kennedy Jr.'s business card telling the world that he is determined to be taken seriously as his own man? Is he disavowing his heritage by not billboarding the fact that he is a president's son—a slain president who is still regarded in mythic terms in the United States?

Of course, the person to ask would be John Jr., since he's the only one who really knows the answers. But based on what he has said in the past about his father and his perceived role as JFK's heir apparent, we can make a reasonable guess that he probably did not give his business card very much thought, nor did he put his omission of certain elements of his august name into any kind of far-reaching context. He simply introduces himself as "John Kennedy"; that's what he has printed on his cards. John is without a doubt fully aware of the archetypal resonance the Kennedy name has in this country and throughout the world. He just doesn't choose to walk around thinking about it.

After all, who in their right mind would want to go through life perceiving himself or herself as a living symbol, anyway?

John F. Kennedy Jr.—don't dare call him "John-John"!—is undoubtedly the most celebrated and watched of all of the twenty-seven surviving members of the Kennedy third generation. The "John-John" nickname was never used by anyone in his family. A reporter overheard JFK repeatedly calling John, saying his name over and over as "John! John!" and assumed that that was what the president and First Lady called the toddler. He wrote it down and, thus, it has survived all these years. In a September 1996 Internet interview on

America Online, John asserted, "No one I know calls me John-John."

John is stunningly handsome and is often spoken of as the last chance for a Kennedy ever again to reside in the White House. Many political insiders and friends of John have privately expressed confidence that John will run for office—perhaps even the presidency—before he reaches his fiftieth birthday.

John *is* the Kennedy of the twenty-first century—and that's a fact whether he ever decides to run for office or not. After all, John is the only Kennedy ever to have an entire *Seinfeld* episode (the infamous "The Contest") revolve around him, and while his uncle Ted has appeared on *Chicago Hope*, John had the privilege of verbally jousting with Candice Bergen on her series *Murphy Brown* to promote the premiere issue of *George*.

As has often been acknowledged in articles and books, John Jr. is not an actor, a musician, a novelist, or a politician (so far), and yet he has *fans*. This is a unique development in the American sociocultural gestalt.

John is renowned because of *who his parents were* and because of the mere *potential* of another JFK someday ending up in the White House—regardless of the fact that John is a relatively young man who has never held an elected office. It should also be acknowledged that John's incredible good looks probably also play some part in endearing him to America's appearance-conscious culture.

John Jr. has been watched by the media since the day he was born. When his father was alive, he and Caroline were cherished as America's favorite toddlers. After his father was assassinated, however, three days before John's third birthday, and the world witnessed the excruciatingly poignant scene of John saluting his father's casket during that solemn November funeral march, John F. Kennedy Jr. has been more than just another president's son. In that brief moment, he became a living representation of his father's truncated administration as well as the period his mother poetically described as "Camelot."

This unceasing attention and the weight of being his father's son has undoubtedly been a burden for John, but he has handled the overwhelming attention with panache, grace, and a confident dignity that bespeaks his mother's strong influence. John has had to deal with the most outlandish and invasive questions on almost a daily basis for his entire life.

Shortly after returning to New York following his top secret marriage to Carolyn Bessette, John was stopped by reporters as he entered his building in TriBeCa after an afternoon of Rollerblading in Central Park. Without so much as a "by your leave," reporters started shouting out, "Is Carolyn pregnant?"

Even though John was reportedly visibly angered by this kind of nonsense, he calmly answered, "I do not comment on our personal life." The reporter persisted with the question, though, until finally John snapped back, "Would you say if *you* were pregnant?" How many people do you know that have to deal with being publicly asked personal questions after an afternoon workout?

It's a wonder this guy smiles at all.

John Jr. was delivered by Cesarean section on Friday, November 25, 1960. He was seventeen days early (his original due date was Monday, December 12, 1960) and the story is told that Jackie conceived John after JFK jokingly told her to shake hands with a minister's wife, and mother of thirteen children, during a campaign stop. "Shake hands with this lady," JFK reportedly said. "Maybe it will rub off on you."

After briefly staying in her father-in-law Joe Kennedy's Palm Beach house with a nanny, Jackie, Caroline, and John moved into the White House permanently in February 1961. One of the few memories John has today of that brief time in the White House was crawling around under his father's desk and also visiting his father every morning before JFK turned to the affairs of state.

And then came November 22, 1963.

Caroline and John were at the White House with nanny Maud Shaw when JFK and Jackie were riding in that open convertible in Dallas. After the word got back to Washington that JFK had been shot and mortally wounded, it fell on Jack's brother, Attorney General Robert F. Kennedy, to inform John of his father's death.

After briefly staying in Averill Harriman's home in Washington, D.C., following the assassination, Jackie bought a house on N Street in Washington, probably thinking that John and Caroline would be better off staying in a town where everyone knew them and where they had friends and routines.

But the assassination changed everything and the two children, as well as their mother, found themselves hounded by reporters and photographers everywhere they went. The situation quickly became intolerable and Jackie decided to move to New York City.

In September 1964, Jackie moved into the Carlyle Hotel in the Big Apple. She and the children lived there for six weeks while their new apartment on Fifth Avenue was being readied to Jackie's specifications. This was the same apartment where John and Caroline would grow up, and where Jackie would eventually die surrounded by her children and her friends.

Jackie strongly believed that her children needed to be raised in as normal an atmosphere as possible and that remaining in Washington, a town where politics is the raison d'être for everyone who lives there, would make normalcy completely untenable.

The year after they all moved to New York, Jackie enrolled John at St. David's School in Manhattan. Jackie personally called the school's headmaster and asked for a tour of the school. He and the staff were reportedly terrified of the encounter, but everything went smoothly. John attended there, along with his cousins Chris Lawford, Steve Smith, William Kennedy Smith, and Tony Radziwill, until 1968, when his mother transferred him to the Collegiate School for Boys, also in New York City. He attended Collegiate until 1976.

When John was sixteen, he transferred to the esteemed Phillips Academy in Andover, Massachusetts, graduating with his high school degree in 1979. Eschewing his family's "college of choice," Harvard, John broke tradition and enrolled in Brown University in Providence, Rhode Island, where he reportedly kept a pet pig in the basement of his fraternity house.

John also tried his hand at acting while in college and was apparently quite good—much to his mother's chagrin. Her husband's alleged dalliance with Marilyn Monroe may have soured Jackie on all things show business. In a February 1997 *Playboy* profile of John Jr. by Jim Dwyer, one of John's Brown University classmates, screenwriter Julie Talen said, "There's a movie in the archives at Brown that was made by a student, and John Kennedy has a big part in it. He was a great actor."

In August 1985, John would also appear in Brian Friel's acclaimed play *Winners*. Jackie and Caroline never attended his six sold-out performances at the Irish Arts Center in Manhattan, although his cousin Kara apparently did go see his performance. Theater patrons had to undergo body searches—probably a New York theater first—and tickets were impossible to acquire, since many of the seats were available by invitation only. John, who was twenty-four at the time, costarred with his then-girlfriend Christina Haag.

Irish Arts Center spokesman Sandy Boyer told Jackie biographer Lester David, "John is an extraordinary and very talented young actor who could have a very successful stage and film career if he wanted it." John would also have a small role in the 1990 film *A Matter of Degrees*, in which he played the guitar and sang the Elvis Costello song "Alison." Interestingly, John was once offered a starring role in a movie about his father in which he would have played JFK Sr. John and Jackie both wisely nixed this tasteless idea.

Throughout his life, John has traveled extensively. He has visited countless foreign lands and even attended school in India for a time. John's foreign "travelog" includes trips to Africa, the Aland Archipelago, Antigua, Argentina, France, Great Britain, Greece, Switzerland, Ireland, Italy, South Africa, Mexico, Guatemala, Russia, and the Caribbean.

John's kayak trip through the Aland Archipelago resulted in an opportunity for him to try his hand at travel writing. Upon his return, he wrote an article for the *New York Times* Travel section about his trip. Here is a passage from John's essay:

> The western winds rose and fell with the sun, and so we slept by day and paddled at night through still water, marveling at the extravagance of a sky where sunrise, sunset and moonrise occur almost simultaneously.

John graduated from Brown in 1983 with a Bachelor's Degree in History. After three years off, a time John spent traveling and deciding what he wanted to do with his life, he enrolled in New York University Law School in Manhattan in 1986. He earned a law degree from the school in three years in 1989, and passed the New York State bar exam after his third try in July 1990.

After graduating law school, John went to work for Manhattan District Attorney Robert Morgenthau. He reportedly hated the job and quit in 1993 after four years. He then began putting together the game plan for his biggest venture yet: his own magazine, the political, cultural, lifestyle, entertainment periodical, *George*, named for one of our homeland's Founding Fathers and, not insignificantly, the man who became our first president.

George began appearing bimonthly in October 1995. The hefty first issue featured a belly-baring Cindy Crawford on its cover and immediately sold out. John Jr. and company published five more bimonthly issues, and in August 1996—five months ahead of schedule—the magazine went to monthly publication. Of his own long-term plans at the time of the magazine's debut, John coyly told reporters at the press conference announcing the magazine, "I hope to end up as president . . . of a very successful publishing venture!"

In April 1996, John and his sister Caroline allowed Sotheby's to auction off many items from their late mother's estate. Neither of the children appeared at the auction, which ultimately raised well over $30 million. Several items pertaining to John were auctioned and the final take was many, many times higher than anyone had expected, once again illustrating the hold Jackie and the Camelot myth have on the American people.

No discussion of John F. Kennedy Jr. would be complete without a look at the many women he has dated throughout his life. Now that he is married, those days are over, but when John was single, he was seen with some of the most beautiful women alive.

One recent book on John listed close to three dozen women he has reportedly been linked with. This lists reads like a "Who's Who" of beauty and brains.

Women John has been rumored to have been involved with include the artist formerly known as Prince's former girlfriend Apollonia; supermodels Audra Avizienis, Julie Baker, Janice Dickinson, Ashley Richardson, Stephanie Schmidt,

Claudia Schiffer, Elle Macpherson, and Cindy Crawford; actresses Sarah Jessica Parker, Melanie Griffith, Catherine Oxenberg, Molly Ringwald, Julia Roberts, Sharon Stone, Brooke Shields, and, of course, Daryl Hannah (his most high-profile romance—politics and Hollywood in one paparazzi picture); rockers Madonna and Sinéad O'Connor; royals Princess Diana, Princess Stephanie of Monaco, and Sarah Ferguson, Duchess of York; not to mention O. J. Simpson's former girlfriend, Paula Barbieri.

John never comments publicly on the women of his life and yet, all of these women have been reported in various periodicals and books as having been involved in some way with the charming John Jr. As with the reasoning behind his business cards, only John, and possibly his wife Carolyn, know for sure!

But all these women are now memories for John.

On Saturday, September 21, 1996, at seven-thirty in the evening, after three months of logistical planning so secret it rivaled some international treaty signings, John Jr. and Carolyn Bessette were married in a forty-five-minute ceremony at the First African Baptist Church on Cumberland Island, Georgia near Hilton Head Island. This tiny "church" was actually an eight-pew wooden chapel without electricity that was built in 1893 by freed slaves after the Civil War. John and Carolyn had less than forty family members and friends at their wedding and the reception was relatively modest.

John and Carolyn's wedding ceremony was double-ring, Roman Catholic, and the service was presided over by Father Charles O'Byrne, a Jesuit deacon from John's mother Jackie's Manhattan parish, the Church of St. Ignatius Loyola.

John's best man was his cousin Tony Radziwill; Carolyn's matron of honor was John's sister, Caroline Kennedy Schlossberg. The couple's flower girls were Caroline's daughters Rose, age eight, and Tatiana, six, and their ring-bearer was the little girls' brother, three-and-a-half-year-old Jack.

Carolyn wore a $40,000, pearl-colored, size six, silk crepe gown that had been designed in Paris especially for her by her friend Narcisco Rodriguez, a designer for Nino Cerutti. She also wore a hair comb that had belonged to Jackie, while John wore his father's watch. Carolyn's bouquet was made up of Jackie's favorite flowers, lilies-of-the-valley, and John's corsage was his father's favorite flower, a blue cornflower.

John's custom-designed blue wool suit was designed by another of Carolyn's friends, fashion designer Gordon Henderson, and John accented the suit with a white piqué vest and a pale blue silk tie. Carolyn worked in the fashion industry at Calvin Klein prior to meeting John, which showed in their wedding design choices.

The couple exchanged matching gold wedding bands that had been designed by John's friend Gogo Ferguson, the woman who also owned the thirty-room Greyfield Inn, the hotel which was the site of John and Carolyn's wedding reception.

There were a couple of funny moments during the ceremony and shortly afterwards. When Caroline Kennedy's son Jack saw Carolyn for the first time dressed in her gown, he asked out loud, "Why is Carolyn all dressed up?" And after the ceremony, as John and Carolyn posed for a few pictures standing by a wooden fence outside the chapel, a horse in a neighboring pasture walked up and began eating Carolyn's bouquet.

Carolyn and John's wedding and reception was deliberately subdued, probably because John knew from experience what would happen if word got out, and he did not want to subject Carolyn and their two families to the media circus that would have undoubtedly occurred if they had married at St. Patrick's Cathedral in New York. (Remember, the family had to have air traffic banned over the Hyannis compound during John's sister Caroline's wedding ceremony.)

The total cost of the affair was estimated at approximately

$600,000, half of which went for fifty private, armed security guards. It was later revealed that John himself picked up the tab for his guests' accommodations, the private jets to shepherd them all back and forth off the island, all the wedding clothes and flowers, as well as paying for all the catering.

Carolyn and John's wedding dinner menu consisted of swordfish, scallops, shrimp, crab, snapper filets, salad, and corn. Their wedding cake was a three-tiered buttercream concoction decorated with fresh flowers, and the song they chose for their first dance was Prince's "Forever in My Life."

Following their wedding, John issued a statement in which he said, "It was important for us to be able to conduct this in a private, prayerful and meaningful way with the people we love."

As expected, the rumors about John and Carolyn began flying immediately after the word got out that the two had wed.

Was there a prenup? Everyone wanted to know, and it wasn't long before the ubiquitous (yet anonymous) "informed sources" revealed to the worldwide media that the two had, indeed, signed a prenuptial agreement and that it had a $10 million cap for Carolyn in the event of a divorce. John has, of course, not responded to questions about such personal matters.

Following their wedding reception, John and Carolyn left for a sixteen-hour flight on a private jet to Istanbul, Turkey, where they stayed for three days at the $500-a-night Ciragan Palace. The happy couple registered as "Mr. and Mrs. Hyannis," yet the tabloid *The Globe* still was able to track them down, photograph them, and run the pictures in the issue of the newspaper that came out the week after the wedding.

Upon their return to New York, John personally and politely asked the ever-present reporters who stood watch outside his building, many of whom he had known for years, to cut his new wife some slack and not hound her all the time the way they did him. He was used to it, he explained, but Carolyn was new to the media attention she had suddenly begun receiving.

None of them, it seems, chose to honor John's request, and Carolyn reportedly was a little taken aback initially by what it meant to be "Mrs. John F. Kennedy Jr." She subsequently made herself scarce for a few months after the wedding. This, of course, fueled all sorts of rumors about her being pregnant, but as of early spring 1997 there was no actual confirmation that John would soon be a daddy.

Today, John is still the editor and copublisher of the magazine *George*.

He has repeatedly described his marriage to Carolyn as strong and has told friends and reporters that he is an extremely happy man.

He is kept very busy handling the day-to-day demands of running a successful magazine and he continues to work out, Rollerblade, attend charity functions, and visit with his family, especially his sister Caroline's kids, one of whom, Jack, is named after John and his father.

Essentially, John F. Kennedy Jr. lives a normal, if privileged life, and he seems to refuse to take himself too seriously.

This does not change the fact that pictures of him and Carolyn are some of the most sought-after celebrity photos in the world. This sometimes makes John and Carolyn's life difficult. Occasionally John shows his temper over this tension, as he did in early 1997 when he confronted a photographer who was guilty of what can only be described as "stalking" John for an entire day.

Stories about John F. Kennedy Jr. are a regular fixture on the TV tabloid shows such as *Hard Copy, Inside Edition*, and *American Journal*. It also seems that he is written about in almost every other issue of the ubiquitous supermarket tabloids.

To date, John has never definitively answered the question, "Do you ever plan on running for office?" Until he does, we will all continue to watch him as he lives the life he was bequeathed when his father was murdered and there was suddenly only one John F. Kennedy in the world.

Seeing as how John is undoubtedly a poised, intelligent, gracious gentleman in a world that wants to pull him in a million directions, perhaps there will come a day when *one* John F. Kennedy is finally enough and John will be known for his achievements simply as John Kennedy, not primarily for being the son of a martyred icon.

THE CHILDREN OF
EUNICE KENNEDY AND
ROBERT SARGENT
SHRIVER

Robert Sargent Shriver III
(b. April 28, 1954)

AKA BOBBY COTTON

We have to measure what we are by what our parents were. Grandpa had things completely wired—Massachusetts, the whole of the East Coast. He had it under control. He was a political consultant, a political action committee, and a media consultant all rolled into one. His only client was his family. He was fanatically dedicated to making it happen. Nobody in this family is ever again going to decide that it's a life-or-death matter whether or not a Kennedy gets elected to something. Even if they did, they can't make it happen anymore. That's what's changed and we might as well admit it.
— BOBBY SHRIVER

One thing that cannot be denied about the Kennedy grand-children is that a great many of them live incredibly interesting lives. Take Bobby Shriver, Eunice Kennedy and Sargent Shriver's oldest child.

Bobby knows some high-profile people. He was the one who introduced his cousin John Jr. to Madonna. Bobby also introduced his sister Maria to Arnold Schwarzenegger.

Bobby, who has dabbled in investments and venture capital projects, was once part-owner of the Baltimore Orioles.

41

At one point in his younger years he worked as a reporter for the Los Angeles *Herald-Examiner*, covering the Rolling Stones for the paper. In the summer of 1972, Bobby worked in Israel on the film version of *Jesus Christ, Superstar*—as a truck driver—and ended up learning that his father Sargent was running for U.S. vice president from a tourist vacationing in Israel. When Bobby was young, he started his own catering business under the name "Bobby Cotton."

But even with all the fame and privilege that came from being Eunice Kennedy's son, Bobby and his siblings' last name was Shriver, not Kennedy, thus, pictures of their JFK cousins John and Caroline were more valuable to photographers when he and his sister Maria were toddlers. In the book *Prince Charming*, Wendy Leigh's fascinating biography of John Jr., a "family friend" is quoted as saying, "Bobby Shriver has a nasty streak that comes out when he's with John" (p. 185). A long-held grudge from their childhood, perhaps?

The stable Shriver family, though, did not let the Kennedy aura overwhelm them. Bobby's father Sargent is fond of reminding people that Shriver is an older name than Kennedy in this country, and that sense of self-confidence and conviction of identity has been a defining touchstone for the Shriver children, including, of course, Bobby III.

Aside from the "fame" disparity between the two branches of the Kennedy clan, Bobby Shriver feels that there are also deeper, more profound differences that can be attributed to each family's attitude toward religion. "My father was brought up in a tradition of German Catholicism, which is a whole different kettle of fish from Irish Catholicism," he explained in *Growing Up Kennedy*. "The German is much more analytical and theologically oriented. The Irish is more emotional and earthy."

The Shrivers would often have religious services in their home, and this commitment to spirituality contributed to the development of a social consciousness that is still obvious today in all of the Shriver children. Bobby has been involved with the group his mother founded, the Special Olympics, from an early age. When he was a young boy, he would help host groups of retarded children his mother would bring to the family estate Timberlawn for five weeks every summer. One of Bobby's most ambitious charitable projects for the organization was the 1987 album *A Very Special Christmas*. This was an album of Christmas songs recorded by pop legends, with the profits going to the Special Olympics. Participants in the project, all of whom donated their talents, included Sting, Bruce Springsteen, Madonna, U2, Annie Lennox, Run-DMC, Whitney Houston, Stevie Wonder, Bryan Adams, Alison Moyet, John Mellencamp, Stevie Nicks, and Bob Seger.

A Very Special Christmas was an enormous success, ultimately providing a $20 million windfall for the Special Olympics.

Bobby attended Phillips Exeter Academy in his adolescent years, graduating from that prestigious institution in 1972. He then attended Yale University and graduated in 1976. Bobby's senior thesis as a undergraduate was on his grandfather, Joe Kennedy. He stayed on in New Haven for the next five years, ultimately graduating from Yale Law School in 1981.

As previously mentioned, Bobby worked on newspapers after law school, moving from a paper in Maryland to the Chicago *Daily News*, then to the Los Angeles *Herald-Examiner*. He reportedly earned $125 a week in LA and insisted on living on his salary alone. His Kennedy family trust fund sat waiting for him, but he wanted to earn a living on his own.

When Bobby Shriver was in his teens, he had a few problems similar to those of his rowdier RFK cousins. In 1970, he was arrested for marijuana possession with his cousin, Bobby Kennedy Jr., and received thirteen months probation. He reportedly sold pot to an undercover narcotics detective posing as a taxi driver. When confronted with his offense, Bobby said, "We never had any *cannabis sativa*. What is *cannabis sativa* anyhow?"

Bobby has a mischievous (and occasionally larcenous) sense of humor. Once, when he was in his teens and visiting his grandmother's Palm Beach House, he used Rose Kennedy's secretary Barbara Gibson's charge card to rent a car (he had already spent his allowance for the next two months). Knowing Gibson would be reimbursed by the Kennedy family anyway, Bobby signed his cousin Joe Kennedy's name to the charge slip.

Today, Bobby lives in Los Angeles and is still involved with the Special Olympics. He has also embarked on a new career as a movie producer. In the early nineties, Bobby developed a story that ultimately became the script for *True Lies*, a hit movie that starred his brother-in-law Arnold Schwarzenegger. He is unmarried and is one of the lesser-known Kennedy grandchildren.

He emerged from childhood relatively unscathed by the damage that the fame of the Kennedy name can cause and is considered today to be one of the most eligible Kennedy bachelors.

Maria Owings Shriver
(b. November 6, 1955)

THE JUGGLER

I had a famous grandfather, a famous father and mother, five famous uncles, and twenty-eight famous cousins. There comes a time for everyone when they have to decide if they are just going to fit in the niche or whether they are going to go out on their own. I wanted to do something that nobody else had done— apart from law school, apart from politics.
— MARIA SHRIVER

Along with Caroline, Maria [is] the other best known Kennedy woman of her generation.
— LAURENCE LEAMER, *The Kennedy Women*

A very revealing story about Maria Shriver emerges from an important 1993 *Good Housekeeping* interview with this famous member of the Kennedy "younger generation."

This story involves, of all people, Fidel Castro: a Communist leader and a thorn in the side of the United States leadership for several decades now.

In October 1962, the United States learned that the Soviet Union had installed offensive missiles with atomic warheads in Cuba, thus creating an ominous and potentially catastrophic threat to the U.S. mainland. The subsequent diplomatic confrontation between the United States and the Soviet Union was ultimately resolved by President Kennedy and is now known as the Cuban Missile Crisis. Kennedy demanded the immediate removal of the missiles from Cuban soil and, after a tense period that included a U.S. air and sea blockade of Cuba, the Soviets agreed to withdraw their nuclear missiles and the world was saved from what could have been a horrible nightmare.

In 1988, NBC correspondent Maria Shriver, looking ahead to the thirtieth anniversary of the Cuban Missile Crisis in 1992, began writing to Fidel Castro, requesting in each letter an interview to discuss what had happened in 1962. She wanted to talk about how Castro felt about the crisis' resolution, as well as what he thought—three decades after the fact—of the actions of her Uncle Jack. For four years Castro ignored Maria's letters.

Finally, in the fall of 1992, Maria decided to resolve the issue once and for all. She intrepidly traveled uninvited to Cuba to confront Castro personally about granting her an interview. She did not know if he would even see her when she arrived, but not only did he and his people acknowledge her presence, on her fifth day there, she was granted an audience with the Communist leader. The meeting resulted in Castro agreeing to an on-camera interview that would be taped the following day.

Maria was thrilled, and probably somewhat relieved. The scheduling of the interview would allow her to be home in time to be with her three-year-old daughter Katherine on her first day at preschool the following week. Maria's husband, film star Arnold Schwarzenegger, was off filming his 1993 movie *Last Action Hero* and would not be able to take Katherine to school if Maria didn't make it home. The child would have had to go to school with a nanny or another family member and, to Maria, this was completely unacceptable.

Then Castro got sick and Maria's interview had to be postponed until the following Monday. This presented a very difficult decision for Maria. As she revealed in the *Good Housekeeping* interview, she told Fidel Castro, "No, for now," and went home to be with her daughter.

We can be certain that Maria knew she was jeopardizing an interview she had worked four years to land. And it's likely that Maria's bosses at NBC were probably not too thrilled with her decision, either. But Maria knew that her daughter needed her, and that fact outweighed any and all career considerations. Thus, Maria left Cuba and was with her daughter Katherine on her first day of school.

Many people would consider Maria's decision ridiculous. To put off an important interview with a world leader just so you can wave to your three-year-old on her first day of school seems the ultimate example of misplaced priorities. But to Maria Shriver and her equally-involved husband, Arnold, raising their children is their most important job, with everything else coming in a distant second or even third place.

Two weeks later, Maria returned to Cuba and completed the interview with Castro. She told journalist Nancy Lloyd that she was amazed that Castro and his staff were not the least bit upset or offended because of her leaving to be with her daughter. In fact, many of the Cubans were actually interested in how things had worked out and whether or not her daughter was doing okay in her new school.

Parents all share a common bond the world over, and it is obvious that Castro and his staff were not at all affronted by Maria's decision. They actually understood and supported it. The defiantly maternal resolve shown by Maria may even have humanized her and endeared her to the feisty Communist, smoothing over some of the inevitable pre-interview tensions always present in these types of high-profile interactions.

❖ ❖ ❖

Maria Owings Shriver was born in Chicago, Illinois, on Sunday, November 6, 1955, the second child (and ultimately only daughter) of Eunice Kennedy and Robert Sargent Shriver.

The Shriver branch of the Kennedy family has often been described as the most stable and grounded of the clan, and if the actions of Maria and her brothers during their growing years are any indicator, then this is undoubtedly true. The foolish and reckless adolescent behavior of some of Maria's cousins did not influence Eunice and Sargent's's little girl: To this day, Maria is on record as stating unequivocally that she has never taken an illicit drug, does not drink, and puts spirituality and the importance of family at the very top of her list of life's priorities.

As did many of her cousins, Maria attended the Stone Ridge Country Day School of the Sacred Heart as a child. She was a third-grade student at the school in November 1963 when her uncle Jack was assassinated in Dallas. Her cousins Kathleen and Courtney (Ethel and RFK's daughters) were also attending the school at this time, and after Ethel received word about the shooting, she picked up the three girls at school and told them about JFK's death. Later in her life, Maria spoke about the deaths of her uncles and her family's reaction to such devastating tragedies:

Our response to things that have happened to the family is to fight back. Your feeling is, "My God, someone got killed." It is impossible to believe that somebody could kill someone so precious to you—could just rip them out of your lives and hurt your cousins so badly. It made you even angrier. Your reaction is, "I'm going to carry on the values they had and the work they did so their loss was not in vain. I'm going to make sure that I make a difference in this world."

After high school, Maria attended Georgetown University in Washington, DC, graduating in 1977 with a degree in American Studies. Her senior undergraduate thesis was about JFK and the role of religion in politics.

Maria has said that she remembers being interested in journalism from around the age of sixteen, and right after graduating from college, she began her pursuit of a career in broadcasting.

Even though she had the last name of Shriver, it was well known that Maria was a Kennedy and that her mother was Eunice, one of the most politically and philanthropically active members of the family. But Maria's family heritage didn't really get her very far when she was just starting out: broadcasting is not a profession where you can "get by," so to speak. Another Kennedy grandchild might be given a corporate position in any number of fields—finance, law, manufacturing—and easily fit in by simply doing his or her job and not making too many mistakes. But being a broadcaster requires a whole new set of qualifications, any one of which, if it is missing, will be instantly noticeable under the cold, unblinking eye of the TV camera. On-air "personalities" need looks, poise, charm, smarts, and the ability to think fast and handle anything thrown their way.

When she was starting out at the age of twenty-two, Maria was (and still is) stunningly attractive, and possessed all the charm and social graces good upbringing and money can bestow. But the standards for being on television, especially for women, are stricter and more demanding than just being from a good family and having an education.

Maria did not have any experience, and she was heavier than the ideal size of a television journalist. She didn't have an agent and her voice and diction were not as polished as they are today. Nevertheless, Barbara Gibson, Rose Kennedy's longtime personal secretary, wrote in *The Kennedys: The Third Generation* that Maria "arrogantly thought she could get work immediately," and noted that Maria holds the distinction of being "the first Kennedy nobody wanted." Maria *was* a Kennedy, however, and thus was given advice by people most of us only have contact with when we watch them on TV. One of these people was family friend Barbara Walters, who gave Maria one important piece of advice: If you want to make it the business of TV journalism, get some experience as soon as possible.

Maria heeded Barbara's counsel and signed up for a Westinghouse TV producer training course. She eventually took her first job in broadcasting as a news writer and producer at a small station, KYW-TV in Baltimore, Maryland. She worked at KYW from 1977 through 1978 before moving to Philadelphia, where she worked as a producer at station WJZ-TV. "I did everything [at WJZ] from carrying coffee, pulling wire copy, and logging tapes to serving on the assignment desk," she told Nadiene Brozan of *The New York Times* in 1985. Maria stayed at WJZ for two years, and while there was responsible for producing their local show, *Evening Magazine*.

WJZ is also where Maria met Oprah Winfrey. The two developed a close relationship that has lasted to this day. Oprah once told the story of coming in to work one morning and finding Maria in the ladies' room splashing cold water on her face. Maria had spent the entire night at the station working on stories for upcoming broadcasts. This was typical of the genuinely driven Maria who, in 1988, told the *Boston Globe*, "People who succeed are disciplined and hard-working. People who get to the top have busted themselves. They've been shot down. But they stick with their goals. I knew I had to emulate that behavior." This kind of determination was not always embraced by others in the media. In the late eighties, *TV Guide* did an article about Maria in which they dubbed her "Maria Striver."

Maria left Philadelphia in 1981 and moved to Los Angeles.

She still did not have an agent, she was still overweight for an on-camera personality, she still had her Boston accent, and she had not yet mastered the art of speaking clearly at a normal rate and *without* using her hands.

Determined and committed, however, Maria spent two months working on her own personal makeover. She dieted and lost weight. She studied voice with a diction coach. Finally, after her transformation, Maria felt she was ready for national exposure. She found it in late 1981 when she was hired as a national reporter on a syndicated show, *PM Magazine*, and worked on a variety of stories for it until 1983.

Maria's visibility on *PM Magazine* resulted in a 1983 offer from *CBS News* in Los Angeles for a job as a news reporter. Maria accepted this job and worked as a national correspondent until September 1985, when she was offered her highest profile job so far: that of coanchor on the third-placed daily morning show, *CBS Morning News*. Maria received the same billing and pay as her cohost Forrest Sawyer, a first for a woman in network news, and the ratings rose dramatically when the two took over the show. But *CBS Morning News* had bigger problems than just the need for better hosts, and the show was ultimately canceled a year after Maria was brought on board.

Maria left CBS in September 1986 and moved to NBC, where she coanchored the weekend edition of *Nightly News*, as well as the Sunday *Today* show. She has been with NBC ever since and has helmed her own series of periodic specials called *First Person with Maria Shriver*, as well as being one of the regular correspondents for *Dateline NBC*.

Maria has always had an elevated agenda for her TV specials. She has always understood the importance of ratings, but she has kept her sights set on something more than just popularity, as evidenced by Maria's comment reported in the book *The Kennedy Women*:

When I started these prime-time specials, it was always with an eye, "Well, if I put on somebody like Michael Jordan or Danny DeVito, people might tune in." But I could also put two other stories that they wouldn't necessarily see in prime time that would become something that they would be interested in and it would have a social conscience.

In the late eighties, Maria also tackled some fairly serious topics in a series of news specials she conceived, wrote, and reported. Notable productions from this period included "The Baby Business," "Men, Women, Sex, and AIDS," "Women Behind Bars," "Wall Street: Money, Greed, and Power," and "God Is Not Elected." Maria also did an important piece called "Fatal Addiction," for which she won the 1990 Christopher Award. Also that year, she was awarded an Exceptional Merit Media Award by the National Women's Political Caucus.

Throughout the period from 1977 through her stint on the *CBS Morning News*, Maria was exclusively dating mega-movie star and world-class bodybuilder Arnold Schwarzenegger. The two had met at the Robert F. Kennedy Pro-Celebrity Tennis Tournament. Arnold had been invited by Maria's brother Bobby Shriver, and he and Rosey Greer had great fun being beaten at tennis by a bunch of ten-year-olds. Maria was immediately charmed by Arnold's good nature and obvious sense of humor, and she asked to be introduced to him. The two hit it off immediately.

Maria and Arnold experienced one of those instantaneous connections that some call "love at first sight," and their attraction to each other was obvious to everyone who witnessed their meeting and subsequent bonding.

But this was one weird union: Arnold Schwarzenegger was an Austrian immigrant with a heavy accent who was known around the world as a "pumped up" bodybuilder and a former Mr. Universe. His book and movie *Pumping Iron* were enormous successes at the time, and he had branched out into other business ventures. More movies, including the phenomenally successful films *The Terminator, Twins,* and *Total Recall,* were on the horizon.

Arnold ultimately became a U.S. citizen, but even though he was dating a woman from a family that essentially defined Democratic liberalism in the twentieth century, he registered as a *Republican.* Maria was apparently not bothered in the least by their political differences and has commented in the past that even though he was with the GOP, most of Arnold's friends were Democrats. And in early 1997, Maria told the New York *Daily News,* "[My husband] is far more liberal than people realize."

Arnold was definitely not someone people would expect one of the descendants of a Democratic political dynasty to fall in love with, but as Maria has admitted, none of this mattered. "I was really crazy about Arnold from the beginning," Maria told *Good Housekeeping.* "I thought [he] was interesting and I was impressed by his sense of humor," she recalled in *The Kennedy Men.*

Arnold proposed to Maria during a summer 1985 visit to his hometown of Thal, Austria. They had dated for nine years by the time they were wed at the Church of St. Francis Xavier on Sunday, April 27, 1986 in Hyannis Port.

Their wedding was a typical Kennedy affair. There were almost five hundred people invited, and the guest list was a "Who's Who" of high-profile celebrities from the worlds of show business, journalism, and of course, politics. Partygoers included Oprah Winfrey, Andy Williams, Abigail "Dear Abby" Van Buren, Tom Brokaw, Diane Sawyer, Art Buchwald, Grace Jones, Quincy Jones, Andy Warhol, Susan St. James, and Barbara Walters, along with, of course, a farrago of famous Kennedys, ranging from Caroline and John to Ted and Jackie.

Maria wore a muslin silk and lace Marc Bohan wedding gown with an eleven-foot train, and during the ceremony Oprah read the Elizabeth Barret Browning poem, "How Do I Love Thee?" Music at the church included the sacred song "Ave Maria," as well as "Maria" from *West Side Story*. The Kennedy family went into overdrive regarding security for the wedding, going so far as to have all air traffic around the Kennedy family compound banned for a two-mile radius from ten in the morning until six that evening.

Maria and Arnold's eight-tier wedding cake weighed an astonishing 425 pounds and stood seven feet high. As a wedding gift, Arnold gave Maria's parents a specially-commissioned Andy Warhol portrait of their daughter. "I'm gaining a wife and you're gaining a painting," he jokingly told them.

Arnold and Maria's first child, Katherine Eunice, was born three years later, on December 13, 1989. Christina Aurelia followed two years afterwards, and then, in 1993, came Arnold and Maria's first son, Patrick.

In early 1997, Maria, then forty-one and pregnant with her and Arnold's fourth child, was hospitalized for nearly a month at St. John's Hospital in Santa Monica, California, due to a problem called hyperemesis that prevented her from keeping down food and fluids. She was fed intravenously while her doctors worked to control the problem. She was released from the hospital in early March. While hospitalized, Maria was visited frequently by her parents, Eunice and Sargent Shriver, as well as her husband Arnold and their three children. She remained on a leave of absence from her duties at NBC, and news reports indicated that her doctor would be the one to determine when she could go back to work. On September 27, Christopher Sargent Shriver Schwarzenegger was welcomed into the world by his loving family and their friends.

Maria Shriver and Arnold Schwarzenegger have a strong marriage and a happy family. Maria is still very close to her parents and siblings and has said that she calls them all every day.

Maria Shriver has built a fabulous career in broadcasting that she still devotes a great deal of time to, and she seems to be a shining example of the woman who can have it all: career, marriage, children, and family closeness.

She visited her Aunt Jackie Onassis on her deathbed and she and Arnold were on the plane that carried Jackie's coffin to Arlington National Cemetery. She was the cherished granddaughter that inherited her grandmother Rose's treasured three-strand pearl necklace. She is deeply involved in the organization formed by her mother, the Special Olympics, and she usually makes an appearance at the annual event in support of the cause. And since Maria is from a family which considers politics the "family business," she has also helped out at rallies for her cousins and has worked on her uncle Ted's senatorial reelection campaigns.

Maria and Arnold collect fine art and live a glamorous life that merges Hollywood, TV, and politics into one incredibly high-profile picture. Maria Shriver seems to be completely successful at juggling a great many responsibilities and obligations—and doing it all with a warmth and charm that has endeared her to not only those who know her personally but also to those who watch her on TV. But it is not as easy as it all seems.

"As much as women want to say we're like guys," she told *Good Housekeeping*, "there's a big difference. Nothing happened to my husband's career after we had children. If anything, it got bigger. But everything about my life changed dramatically. I had two children very close together, and they became my focus [instead of the job.]"

But Maria Shriver being who she is, there was no way she could completely lose focus on her career. Before she wed Arnold, she told Kennedy biographers Harrison Rainie and John Quinn, "I love my work and want to stay at it, but I am insanely jealous of my friends who are married and have children." She does love her work and honestly feels she can do some good with her TV specials and interviews. Because NBC considers her a valuable asset to their network, they have accommodated her lifestyle changes and allow her to work for the most part out of an office in her home in Pacific Palisades, and also allow her to bring her kids with her to the studio when she needs to do on-camera work.

Maria Shriver seems to have it all, but those who are close to her know that none of it came easy for this young woman who was accused of trading on her family name and who was probably held to a higher standard. She persevered, however, and today is happy and fulfilled—if unbelievably busy and usually exhausted.

Maria's friend Oprah Winfrey, a woman who has achieved great things and been phenomenally successful in her own right, actually looks to Maria as a role model. "I love her," Oprah told *Good Housekeeping*'s journalist Nancy Lloyd, "because she represents the best of what we can be as women. That she's been able to create this sense of balance between her family and work [makes her] a wonderful role model— and I intend to follow her example."

Maria Shriver has come a long way from playing the lead in *Cinderella* when she performed plays with her Kennedy cousins when she was a kid. But when you consider that Maria, like Cinderella, ultimately ended up living a wonderful fairy-tale lifestyle, she's really not too far away at all from those halcyon years when a little dark-haired girl put on a pretend glass slipper and wished for her own Prince Charming.

Maria Shriver is a convincing example of what can happen when a dream is pursued—even if it means a little clever juggling now and then.

Timothy Perry Shriver

(b. August 29, 1959)

THE PRIEST

*We grew up where important was fun, and fun was important.
That's not to say people don't recreate in dumb ways—go to
the movies, twiddle their thumbs, whatever you do. But the challenge of making things better was important. Even playing a
game of stickball could be significant, at the same time it was
a pleasure. When you come to realize that what you are doing
is important, you become more committed to it.*
    —TIM SHRIVER, in *U.S. News & World Report*

Timothy Perry Shriver—Eunice Kennedy and Sargent
Shriver's middle child—is married to Linda Potter and they
have children. So, unless the Catholic Church has made an
earth-shattering exception for Tim, there is no way the subtitle
of this chapter could be accurate.

But it is, in a way.

Tim's nickname of "the Priest" was given to him by his
cousins and friends who saw in him a selfless realization of
the Christian ideal of love and social responsibility.

Tim has expounded on what motivates him:

Religion is an important defining characteristic for all
of us, and deeds are only part of what you can do.

That's important, but we were taught that you have to be a loving, caring Christian person to make it worthwhile. I realized that to make up for what my family has and to pay for it, one does other things to help people one way or another.

Tim also said that he enjoys Catholicism and that he has learned a lot from studying the faith. He enjoys going to Mass and is clearly one of the more spiritually-driven of the younger generation of Kennedys. He believes that his religion empowers him, but also is confident that, "Those who don't practice their faith as much as I are just as much a part of the divine plan as I am." Tim has been known to collect religious artifacts and often quotes from the Bible.

As an young man, Tim practiced what he preached. In 1981, he tutored a group of Lorton prison inmates who wanted to earn their high school equivalency diplomas. In the early eighties, he worked in New Haven, Connecticut, for not one but two social service agencies, one for sexually abused children, and one for gifted poor children. During the summer of 1982, during his junior year in college, he and his cousin John Jr. tutored underprivileged children in English at the University of Connecticut. Tim reportedly came down hard on cousin John when he sensed he was shirking his tutoring duties a little.

Tim attended St. Alban's School in Washington, DC, graduating in 1977, and then went on to Yale University, from which he graduated in 1981. He ultimately earned a master's degree in Spirituality and Education from Catholic University in DC.

Growing up, Tim and his sister Maria visited Aristotle Onassis' island, Skorpios, with cousins John and Caroline, and toured Russia with the other Shrivers. Also, John Jr.

and Tim once took a diving trip to the Caroline Islands together and even traveled together to Rabinal, Guatemala, in 1976 to help earthquake victims there.

Today, Tim has his doctorate in education and is president of the Special Olympics, the organization founded by his mother, Eunice, and supported by the entire Kennedy family.

In 1995, Tim was honored at the opening ceremonies of the Special Olympics in New Haven by President Bill Clinton, who also made special mention of Tim's mother Eunice, acknowledging her "energy" and commitment to the Special Olympics. President Clinton also thanked Sargent Shriver, then singled out Tim "for doing such an outstanding job as president of these 1995 games."

Tim married Linda Potter on Memorial Day, 1986. They have four children: Rose, Timothy, Samuel, and Kathleen.

Tim could have maintained a high profile in his job. The Special Olympics is an organization known around the world. Yet Tim Shriver keeps a relatively low profile, preferring anonymity to the spotlight. His mother Eunice is the "Shriver" who comes to mind when the Special Olympics is mentioned, and yet Tim is the "commander-in-chief" of the organization, responsible for much of the organization's activities. Except for the annual games themselves, however, we don't often hear from Tim. And that's apparently the way he likes it.

He reportedly never liked campaigning because he didn't like being looked upon as "the Nephew." Even though he enjoys socializing, he has never sought out the "party lifestyle" in places like Hyannis Port, New York, Boston, or Washington. He works hard and stays out of the limelight.

Also, there do not seem to be any skeletons in Tim Shriver's closet. The drug abuse, alcohol problems, rehab scenarios, and legal troubles common in the lives of some of his cousins are nowhere to be found in Timothy Perry Shriver's personal biography. He is spiritually driven and believes he has a purpose in life: to help others.

Overall, Tim's family nickname of "the Priest" seems right on the money.

Mark Kennedy Shriver

(b. February 17, 1964)

THE COMMUNITARIAN

I don't want to be in the race, Daddy.
— MARK SHRIVER, to his father at a swim
meet when he was a child.

After opting out of a competitive Kennedy swimming race
when he was kid, Mark Kennedy Shriver went on to compete
in a different kind of race and achieve the notoriety of being
the only one of the five Shriver children to enter politics.

In 1994, at the age of thirty, Mark was elected to the
Maryland House of Delegates after claiming to have knocked
on more than twelve thousand doors in his home district of
Montgomery County during his campaign. Prior to the November 8, 1994 election, Mark told *People* magazine, "I'm having my shoes resoled for the sixth time." He also revealed his
cardinal rule for door-to-door campaigning, apparently
learned from firsthand experience: "Don't walk on people's
lawns. They get really mad."

There is a genuine paradox in Mark's political success. He
reportedly never seemed to feel comfortable with the Kennedy

political/personal ideology of winning at any cost, and he pointedly told *People* that he deliberately avoided trying to capitalize on either the Shriver or the Kennedy names during his run for office. And yet, he ran, he won, and he is now one of the few Kennedy grandchildren in public office. This, despite his claim that, "We didn't talk politics my entire childhood," truly unusual for the family of a Kennedy sister.

Mark, the second youngest of Sargent and Eunice's kids, graduated from Georgetown Prep School in 1982 and went on to the College of the Holy Cross, graduating in 1986 with a degree in history.

Mark, who was described in *Growing Up Kennedy* as "a hearty, bluff Irishman," has always been involved in sports and grew up sailing, playing tennis, rugby, and absolutely loving baseball, a passion which ultimately led to a 1982 front-office job with the Baltimore Orioles. Orioles owner Edward Bennett Williams, a Shriver family friend, got Mark this baseball-lover's dream job.

In 1988, Mark created an innovative program called CHOICE, which provided tutors and mentors for underprivileged, inner-city kids in Baltimore. Today, "mentoring" is advertised by big-name TV stars and is one more facet of the burgeoning "volunteerism" movement, a trend Mark seemed to have foreseen and may have actually had a hand in establishing.

Mark, who is a member of the Maryland General Assembly, is married to Jeanne Ripps, and is also an account executive with American Express. Mark and Jeanne live in Bethesda, Maryland, and have a gorgeous white dog named Buddy.

Mark espouses what he describes as a "serious commitment to public policy." In fact, he has even coined a word to describe his approach to social problems: "Communitarian," a hybrid of the words "community" and "humanitarian," a strategy he hopes will more actively involve people in a community who want to help solve their own problems — another apparent forerunner of "volunteerism."

The Shriver branch of the Kennedy tree has bloomed with energetic young people who are deliberately trying to make a difference — Tim, with the Special Olympics; Anthony, with his organization Best Buddies; Maria, with her public service TV features; Bobby's *Very Special Christmas* charitable project for the Special Olympics; and Mark, with his "Communitarian" work.

As we have seen, Mark is the Shriver now in politics. It would be ironic, indeed, if this philanthropically-driven family was the division of the Kennedy family from which the next "Kennedy" president came forth. The irony would lie in the fact that the next "Kennedy president" would be named President Shriver. And if this happened, Eunice Kennedy Shriver would become the first woman in history to have had both a brother *and* a son as president of the United States.

So far, Mark has not yet publicly expressed any interest in running for higher office, but he is in the perfect position to try, if he should so decide. In the meantime, he works diligently in the Maryland House of Delegates, envisioning a time when the community compassionately helps its own, and doing everything in his power to make that vision a reality.

Anthony Paul Kennedy Shriver

(b. July 20, 1965)

THIS BUDDY'S FOR YOU

The big thing to remember is to have patience and compassion and to have your heart open.
—ANTHONY SHRIVER, in *People* magazine, talking about the mission goal of his organization, Best Buddies

The timing could not have pleased Anthony Shriver.

Just before he planned to announce that he was going to be yet another Kennedy cousin running for political office, all hell broke loose with two of his RFK cousins.

In April 1997, Joe Kennedy II's ex-wife Sheila Rauch published a book that blasted Joe from his Kennedy curls to the soles of his politician's shoes for successfully getting their long-dead marriage annulled by the Catholic Church. Sheila was in all the papers and even talked to Diane Sawyer on *Prime Time Live*. Immediately, Joe, who planned on running for the Massachusetts governor's seat in 1998, found himself tap-dancing all over this story, apologizing to anyone who would listen, and trying to put a spin on this embarrassment which would destroy his chances at winning the governor's race the following year.

The "Joe/Sheila" story was bad. Then came the Michael Kennedy debacle.

Even though no charges were pressed against Michael, it is apparently true that he did, indeed, have a five-year affair with his family's babysitter that began when the girl was only fourteen, opening him up to statutory rape allegations and giving the tabloids their front page story for several weeks to follow. [See the chapters on Joe II and Michael.]

And in the midst of all this hullabaloo, Anthony Shriver— Eunice and Sargent's youngest child—announced at the end of April of 1997 that he wanted to be mayor of Miami Beach, Florida. The news coverage of Anthony's announcement all began by talking about Joe and Michael's recent scandals. Anthony was painted with the brush of infamy simply because he was part of the family in which Joe and Michael also "resided."

The *New York Post* began their coverage of Anthony's announcement with, "While the Kennedys reel over their latest scandals, another family member yesterday said he hopes to further expand their political dynasty" The *Post* interviewed South Florida political commentator Jack Cole of WJNO radio. Cole was less than thrilled with Anthony's announcement and said, "I don't know where these Kennedy men get their *chutzpah*. I mean, what has Anthony ever done for Miami Beach? It seems like a strange time to express interest in an elective office, but I'm not saying for one minute that he isn't going to win."

Anthony's public remarks quoted in the *New York Post* after his announcement were, admittedly, somewhat unusual. He started out conventionally with, "I grew up in a family that viewed politics as a tremendously noble calling," but then veered into the realm of non sequitur by concluding, "I love the beach."

In addition to having to deal with the fallout from his two cousins' sordid troubles, Anthony also had to cope with some of his past "indiscretions" plastered all over the newspapers now that he was a political wannabe and fair game for the media scandal hounds.

Post columnist Neal Travis, in his widely-read "New York" column, was one of the first to write about an incident that took place at Donald Trump's Mar-a-Lago mansion in Palm Beach, Florida, when Anthony was twenty-eight years old. The story goes that Anthony, who was not one of the eight hundred lucky ones invited to a big bash at the Donald's mansion, crashed the party and reportedly behaved in a rude and boisterous manner. As he was leaving the grounds, Anthony then drove his Jeep into a seventy-year-old palm tree (the tree ended up firewood, as the story goes) and the police were called. Donald Trump not only refused to press charges against Anthony, but also did not demand reparations for any of the damage the Kennedy scion caused. The point Travis and others made was that if Shriver does get elected mayor, he may have Donald to thank for it, since the Mar-a-Lago incident could have jeopardized any of Anthony's political plans—if Anthony had ultimately ever been charged with anything.

Anthony Shriver attended Georgetown Preparatory School (as did his brother Mark and his cousins Chris, Joe II, and Bobby Kennedy Jr.) and briefly dated actress Tatum O'Neal (as did his cousins Chris and Michael Kennedy).

He went on to graduate from Georgetown University, and while in college formed the organization that embodied all of the principles espoused by his mother and father regarding the mentally retarded. Anthony started Best Buddies in his junior year of college, a volunteer organization that seeks to help the mentally handicapped more easily fit into mainstream society with the assistance and friendship of "best buddies," volunteers who take them out for day trips and excursions.

Best Buddies go to malls, restaurants, the movies, and

their stated goal is to make other people feel less threatened and more comfortable when they come upon a mentally handicapped person out in public.

"Part of our mission is to make it so people won't stare," Anthony told *People* magazine in February 1995. "So when you go downtown or into church, they're used to having people with mental retardation in there."

Anthony's personal interest in helping the mentally handicapped stems from his affection for his aunt Rosemary, his mother Eunice's mentally handicapped sister who lives in a convent in Wisconsin. Anthony admits to always having had a great rapport with his aunt. "I just find Rosemary to be a very moving and inspirational figure," he said in *The Kennedy Women*. "It's hard to describe. But I think her smile and her efforts just from point A to point B, as little as that may be, it's very motivational and energizing and it reorients you back to sort of the presence of your heart in a lot of ways."

Anthony got the idea for Best Buddies after he "saw a lot of my buddies sitting around watching soaps and partying, not doing a whole heck of a lot in the community," he told *People*. "I figured it wouldn't take a huge effort to integrate someone into their daily routine," he said, and the first Best Buddies rally he organized drew fifty volunteers, all of whom he paired with people from group homes and other facilities for the mentally handicapped.

Anthony ultimately ended up helping start Best Buddies chapters at other colleges, and by 1995, Best Buddies International Inc. had branches in thirty-seven states, several foreign countries, and had spun off into high school groups, corporate groups, and a division that helps the handicapped find jobs. By then, the organization had also become Anthony's full-time job, and the highly-regarded group boasted such celebrity supporters as artists Roy Lichtenstein and William Wegman, and fashion designers Gianni Versace and Calvin Klein.

Anthony reportedly visits his aunt Rosemary frequently,

and even went so far as to have a room added on to his Miami Beach house especially for when she visits Florida.

Anthony Shriver has always been very aware of the profound influence his parents have had on his personal ideology and on his life in general.

As we have seen, the Shriver children were raised somewhat differently than some of the other Kennedy cousins. The Shriver kids grew up knowing where the boundaries were—they were disciplined by parents who looked to their religion for answers and who refused to tolerate laziness or self-indulgence in their children.

Anthony has admitted he found it "daunting" working down the hall from his formidable mother when Best Buddies was just getting off the ground, but he has also spoken of the time he asked his father Sargent why he went to church every day. "Because I'm so weak," his father told him, "and I need so much help."

This philosophy obviously contributed to Anthony's adult selflessness and relentlessly positive attitude. His wife Alina told *People*, "Everyone who's around him knows he's an optimist. Anthony always sees the better side of things."

Today, Anthony is still very active with Best Buddies and recently was part of an investment group that purchased the Larkin Hospital in South Miami. He is married to Cuban-born Alina Mojica and they have three children, Teddy, an eight-year-old from Alina's previous marriage; Eunice, who was three in 1997; and little Francesca, a year younger than her sister.

Alina and Anthony met in 1991 at a Best Buddies fundraiser and she fully supports his commitment to the organization. She is on the board of directors of Best Buddies and is usually by his side at many of the functions surrounding the group, of which there are many.

If Anthony Shriver wins the 1998 mayoral election in Miami Beach—and there's a solid chance he will—he will be yet one more Kennedy grandchild entering public office. And then his mother Eunice, already pleased by his many achievements, will have one more thing to be proud of.

The Children of
Patricia Kennedy
and Peter Lawford

Christopher Kennedy Lawford
(b. March 29, 1955)

THE ACTING KENNEDY

We were all, every one of us, raised to be President. . . . The Presidency is in our system and we can't get it out. We can't get free enough of it to consider doing something else with our lives.
—CHRIS LAWFORD

Our family loves [Chris's acting career], and his father would have been very happy and excited, same as I am.
—CHRIS's mother, Pat Kennedy

As a child, Christopher Kennedy Lawford—the son of Pat Kennedy and actor Peter Lawford—not only had to deal with the burden of being a Kennedy, he also had to grow up as the son of a world-famous Hollywood actor who was more interested in young women, booze, and drugs than being involved in his children's lives.

Chris' parents were divorced when Chris was ten, and his mother immediately moved back to the East coast with Chris and his three sisters, Sydney, Victoria, and Robin. Peter Lawford remained in California. The end result of this split was that Chris and his siblings joined the sad contingent of Kennedy cousins who only had one parent in their lives. JFK and RFK's kids both lost their dads through assassination; Chris lost his through divorce. *How* it happened did not matter, though: Chris and his sisters still grew up essentially fatherless. Despite his father's lack of presence as a role model, however, the force of the Hollywood half of Chris' heritage has been an important part of his life.

Chris felt pulled in several directions during his adolescent years. On one hand, he felt drawn to his father's career. Another part of him told him he was a Kennedy and therefore he should become a lawyer and go into politics. At times, he grappled with what being "a Kennedy" meant, often coming to the conclusion that being one did not always mean working for a greater good. "I used to think that what my family did was involved with a desire to serve the country," he told Peter Collier and David Horowitz in *The Kennedys: An American Drama*. "Now I keep asking myself what was it in my grandfather that made him push the family so hard and cause us all such tragedy?"

Trying to understand the Kennedy dynasty did bring Chris to some conclusions, including the realization that "[T]he Kennedy story is really about karma, about people who broke the rules and were ultimately broken by them."

Chris Lawford holds the distinction of being the only Kennedy grandchild whose delivery was attended by his grandmother, Rose Kennedy, who Chris has repeatedly described as "very, very special."

Chris was Pat and Peter's first child, and the whole experience of being new parents was extremely disruptive and overwhelming for the famous couple. One of the first things they did upon Pat's return from the hospital with Chris was to rent a separate apartment two doors down from their home for a full-time nanny to live in with Chris. His parents would visit him there instead of caring for him on a daily basis.

Chris lived in Santa Monica as a child, but frequently visited the Kennedy compound and his twenty-eight cousins in Hyannis Port. In 1991, Chris reminisced to *People* magazine about those halcyon, pre-heroin, pre-Dallas days, remembering selling "Kennedy sand" (ordinary Hyannis Port beach sand) for a dollar a bag to Kennedy-crazed tourists.

After his parents' breakup in the mid-sixties and his move with his mother to New York, Chris attended St. David's School in Manhattan with his cousin John Jr., but did not follow John to Collegiate and Andover. While at St. David's, Chris roomed with his RFK cousin, Bobby Jr. Chris has admitted that he always felt that he lived in Bobby Jr.'s shadow as an adolescent and that there were times when he felt as though he was less a Kennedy because he didn't have the magic last name. In fact, Chris admitted, "I went through a period in my teens and early twenties when I would say, 'I want out. I wish I could go off and be somebody else.' "

Part of Chris' angst in his formative years was definitely due to his relationship, or perhaps nonrelationship, with his father, Peter Lawford. They didn't see each other that often in the first few years after the divorce, but as Chris got older, he and his father did have more contact with each other—and their get-togethers were not wholly beneficial to Chris. "[W]e were more friends than father-son," he told *People* in 1991. "I loved my father, but it was weird. He went out with women who were my age."

A typical example of the bizarre way father and son interacted with each other was what went on during Chris' 1970 visit to the Vancouver, British Columbia, set for his dad's CBS miniseries *The Deadly Hunt*.

Chris, who would be sixteen the following March, and who had been using drugs since his prep school days, was staying with Peter in Los Angeles for the summer. He flew to Vancouver and was met at the airport by his dad's new wife, Mary. Once they got to the set, the three of them frequently smoked pot together. They smoked so much that it got to the point where John Newland, the film's director, was reportedly angry and concerned about the drug use, even though Peter limited his smoking to times when he wasn't shooting.

Peter obviously thought nothing of getting high with his teenaged son. This attitude more than likely contributed to Chris' later, quite serious drug problems. Incredibly, Peter's twenty-first birthday present to Chris was a supply of cocaine. "Thanks for the gift," Chris wrote to his father in a thank-you note. "Unfortunately it was not one I could hold on to for very long."

Another time, Chris was out to dinner with his father and others, and when the bill came, Peter told his son he didn't have any money. He persuaded Chris to charge the tab on his mother Pat Kennedy's credit card. Later in the evening, Peter pulled out three one-hundred-dollar bills and gave them to Chris to score him some cocaine. This stunt genuinely angered Chris, and he has said that he had to restrain himself from punching his father.

There are many stories of Chris' problems with drugs, including incidents at Pat Kennedy's Manhattan apartment, when he and his cousin David Kennedy moved into the empty apartment for their drug parties. Chris was closest to David of all his cousins and was devastated by his untimely drug overdose death. As recently as 1991, Chris couldn't talk freely about David. When he did speak with a *People* journalist, he simply said, "It's really hard when you lose someone you care about." As an adolescent, he was expelled from Middlesex Academy for drug use, and in 1979, at the age of twenty-four, he was busted for heroin possession in a Roxbury, Massachusetts, ghetto. Shortly thereafter, in 1980, he was arrested for impersonating a doctor in Aspen, Colorado. He was trying to convince a pharmacist to fill a bogus Darvon prescription and the suspicious druggist called the cops.

It was later that year when the time bomb that was Chris' drug use exploded. At the age of twenty-five he ended up in a Boston hospital fighting pneumonia and a collapsed lung, both of which were due to his drug abuse. "I was near the end," he said in *Growing Up Kennedy*. "Nothing. Checking out. I mean, my heart almost stopped beating. Something had to change and I knew it." In 1991, Chris would tell *People* magazine, "I never intended for drugs to wreck my life, but that's exactly what happened." It took Chris a few more years to get totally clean, but by the mid-eighties, he was off drugs completely.

After graduating from Tufts University, he enrolled in Fordham Law School, but his drug use was still too destructive and he had to drop out after only a few months. He moved back to Boston, where he met his future wife, Jeannie Olsson, a stunning brunette who was working at the time for *New York* magazine and who was also battling her own drug problem. She was a strong and positive influence on Chris, though, even with her own problems, and they were married in 1984, a month before Chris' father's drug-and-alcohol-induced death. Chris and Jeannie beat drugs together in 1985 after successfully completing an Addictive Behavior Course at Cambridge Hospital in Massachusetts. Today they have three children, Savannah, Matthew, and David, named after Chris' favorite cousin.

Chris ultimately graduated from Boston College Law School in 1983, but abandoned his law career after failing the bar exam. In a comment reminiscent of his cousin John Jr.'s self-effacing remark that he was not "a legal genius" after he failed *his* exam twice, Chris told *People* magazine, "I was just not a legal beagle."

In the past decade, Chris has followed in his father's footsteps by concentrating on his acting career. He has tried *not* to follow his dad's less-than-stellar child-rearing standards, however, by being a superlative father to his and Jeannie's three kids. "He does a lot more than a normal husband would do," his wife told *People*. "That's very important to him."

One of Chris' more notable recent feature film appearances was playing Lieutenant Martins in the 1991 theatrical release *Run*, a very effective action thriller starring Patrick Dempsey and Kelly Preston. Martins is more fully developed than many of the minor characters Chris has played in movies in the past few years. In *The Doors*, for instance, which was released the same year as *Run*, Chris played a *New York Times* reporter, speaking only one line.

Chris Lawford's role in *Run* was an important one, however, and his Lieutenant Martins had the distinction of being the pivotal character who acted as the Dempsey character's champion. He gave a good performance, and the following year began playing the character of Charlie Brent on the soap *All My Children*, a visible and high-profile role.

Chris' other film work includes roles in *The Russia House* (1990); *Impulse* (1990); *Mr. North* (1988); *Jack the Bear* (1993); *Blankman* (1994); *Pulp Fiction* (1994); *Drunks* (1996); the TV-movie *The Abduction* (1996); and *Kiss Me, Guido* (1997), his first independently produced film. His TV work has also included guest shots on *Silk Stalkings* and a role in an episode of HBO's horror series *Tales From the Crypt*, in which he was directed by his cousin-in-law, Arnold Schwarzenegger.

Demonstrating Chris' continued progress at his career, his first feature film as an actor and executive producer, *Kiss Me, Guido*, opened in July 1997.

Chris has an interesting physical appearance, one in which the influences of both the Kennedy and Lawford gene pools can be seen. He has the angular Kennedy facial features as well as the small mouth and pursed lips of his father, Peter Lawford. Not classically handsome, he nonetheless has a charming presence and offbeat look that combine to render

him quite attractive, especially to the many female fans he
acquired during his four years on *All My Children*.

Today, it seems as though Chris Lawford will definitely
be a presence in the TV and film world for many years to
come. There was a time when Chris actually considered getting into politics. As the epigraph to this chapter reveals, the
presidency is an enormous presence in the lives of the Kennedy younger generation. Whether or not Chris ever decides
to run for an elected office, he will always be remembered as
coming from a political family and being the son of one of
the Kennedy women.

In 1994, Chris campaigned for his uncle Ted, describing
the experience as "instinctual." He was playing on *All My
Children* at the time, but he told *People* magazine that he was
helping out "because he's my uncle and I love him and I'd
do anything for him." He also admitted that it was easier to
campaign for someone when you agree with their politics,
which he most assuredly did in the case of Ted Kennedy.
Interestingly, later that year Chris played a mayor in Damon
Wayans' comedy *Blankman*.

Acting seems to be the road Chris is destined to walk.
When Chris' father Peter Lawford died December 25, 1984,
the Christmas morning headline of the Los Angeles *Herald-
Examiner* read, "Peter Lawford Dead at 61." The subhead
read, "Kennedy in-law was last to speak to Marilyn Monroe,"
as if, sadly, Lawford's Hollywood connections were the most
important thing about him. Peter Lawford's Hollywood aura
remained with him while his White House involvement, his
friendships with Jack and the other Kennedys, his marriage
to one of Joe Kennedy's girls, and all his other political dalli-
ances were reduced to two words: "Kennedy in-law."

This is the gene pool from which Chris Lawford emerged.

Only time will tell if the pull of politics can win in a tug-
of-war between Chris' acting career and the political half of
his heritage. John Kennedy Jr. also toyed with the idea of

an acting career, but his mother effectively steered him toward law. Chris Lawford, on the other hand, has been *encouraged* by his mother in the pursuit of an acting career, and his wife is likewise supportive. With all these elements in his favor — acting genes, a clean and sober lifestyle, a supportive family (including his cousin-in-law, Hollywood powerhouse Arnold Schwarzenegger), the odds are greatly in favor of us continuing to see Chris in movies and TV productions for many years to come.

Because even though he is known as "the acting Kennedy," his last name is Lawford; on a marquee, that probably carries more clout.

Sydney Maleia Lawford

(b. August 25, 1956)

FAMILY MATTERS

I, Sydney, take you Peter to be my husband. I promise to be true to you in good times and in bad, in sickness and in health. I will love and honor you all the days of my life.
—SYDNEY LAWFORD's "obey"-less wedding vows,
    as recounted in *The Kennedy Women*

There are many reasons why some of the Kennedy grandchildren choose to stay out of the public eye.

It is true that several of them *have* accepted the fact that, because of who they are, the white hot spotlight of the media follows them wherever they go, recording their every move. These members of the younger generation welcome the attention and have deliberately chosen careers that put them in front of the public on a regular basis. Chris Lawford is an actor; Maria Shriver is on TV; several grandchildren are in politics. But then there are those Kennedy members of the third tier who choose to figuratively wear caps and sunglasses whenever they venture out into our curious world.

When Sydney Lawford was in her teens and twenties, she was most definitely *out there*. A stunningly attractive woman,

Sydney initially had a career as a fashion model, a not-unusual vocational choice for the daughter of one of Hollywood's biggest stars.

She studied at the Tobé-Coburn School of Fashion in New York and had a dark, sultry look that was very appealing, and which kept her busy as a model after her college years.

Today, though, Sydney is a stay-at-home mom in Chevy Chase, Maryland, with four kids and a husband who goes to work every day to support his family. Sydney, who also worked with C-SPAN for a time, has effectively given up her modeling career and opted for domesticity, a choice many previously career-minded women are embracing with passion today.

Why did this daughter of a world-famous movie star—the twenty-six-year-old bride who refused to be "given away," or to include the word "obey" in her wedding vows—choose to give up her high-profile career for relative anonymity in a Maryland suburb, where she is better known as "Mrs. McKelvy" than as "Peter Lawford's daughter"?

There are a couple of incidents from Sydney's personal biography that might have convinced her that a life in the limelight was less than desirable.

One is the ordeal of having to cope with her cousin David Kennedy's drug overdose death in Palm Beach. Sydney and her cousin Caroline Kennedy were the family members who had to identify David's body. The two young women were also questioned by the police and, to this day, there are conflicting accounts of the events surrounding David's death. David's overdose had to have been a traumatic experience for Sydney, and within days following his death, her and Caroline's names were all over the papers; the media were constantly hounding them for comments about the tragedy. This incident, which took place when Sydney was twenty-eight, was probably the straw that broke the Lawford's back, so to speak.

But there was another event in Sydney's life eight years earlier that had to have dramatically illustrated to her just what being famous was all about. She learned that being well known meant that reporters would keep track of your bathroom habits. This embarrassing moment, recounted in the unauthorized biography of Ted Kennedy, Rick Burke's book *The Senator*, occurred in 1976, when Sydney was twenty and on the campaign trail with her uncle Ted.

The Ted Kennedy team was riding on a campaign bus that did not have any bathrooms and, of course, nature called out to Sydney—at a most inopportune time. Her uncle Ted pleaded with her to try and hold it until their next stop, but Sydney just couldn't. "Uncle Ted, I can't hold it any longer!" she finally exclaimed, and Ted reluctantly ordered the bus to pull over onto the side of a New Hampshire highway. Ted asked his aide, author Rick Burke, to take Sydney up into the woods to do her business. He walked her up a hill as the Secret Service stood guard around the bus and kept an eye on Sydney, and everyone waited as the young woman ran deeper into the woods to do her "Number One."

As Rick waited, Sydney suddenly cried out, "I don't have any toilet paper!"

Rick went back to the bus, found some, and made a female campaign worker bring it up to Sydney, who finished up and returned to the bus.

This would just be an amusing anecdote of life on the campaign trail if it wasn't for one painfully embarrassing element: because it was *Ted Kennedy* on the trail, hordes of reporters were following behind his campaign caravan, stopping when he stopped, and recording every moment of his political "expedition." And so, because they were all there, the press recorded every moment of Sydney's embarrassing bathroom stop.

Whether or not these two moments from Sydney's life affected her enough to influence her decision to drop out of the spotlight is probably known only to Sydney and those close to her. But it's interesting to speculate, and whatever the truth is, these two episodes could not have made her think warmly of the media and may have contributed to her ongoing deliberate avoidance of fame and publicity.

Sydney Maleia Lawford was named for Peter Lawford's father, General Sydney Lawford, a British World War I hero. As a child, Sydney attended all the right schools—the Fox-croft School, the Convent of the Sacred Heart—before enter-ing the University of Miami. She also studied at Franklin College in Lugano, Switzerland, before returning to the States to study fashion at the aforementioned Tobé-Coburn School in Manhattan.

Sydney was only nine when her mother Pat and her father Peter Lawford divorced. At Pat's urging, Sydney tried to maintain contact with her father over the years via cards, letters, telegrams, and other missives. Sydney reportedly adored her father and her childhood bedroom was plastered with pictures of Peter from many of his movies.

Sydney, who began collecting her Kennedy trust fund when she was twenty-one, has always had a strong sense of family. She has always been very close with her cousin Caro-line and likewise had a warm and close relationship with her grandmother Rose when she was alive. In fact, Sydney was the granddaughter who personally accompanied Rose on her final flight to Hyannis Port in 1984.

On September 17, 1983, Sydney married TV producer Peter McKelvy at Our Lady of Victory Church, followed by a big Kennedy, Hyannis Port reception. Grandmother Rose, who was ninety-three, attended this special wedding, and some of the guests included Oleg Cassini and Norman Mailer. Sydney's brother Chris read from the scriptures during the ceremony, and, on her way out of the church, Sydney stopped at her father's pew to warmly embrace and kiss her dad.

Today, Sydney is at home raising her children—four McKelvy boys, James, Christopher, Patrick, and Anthony—who are members of the fourth generation of the Kennedy dynasty.

It remains to be seen if Sydney will ever decide to forgo anonymity and return to either the broadcasting world, or the fashion industry. That decision, though, is probably years away, and in the meantime, she is extremely busy with raising her children and enjoying her life as a Kennedy grandchild with a last name that is most assuredly not "Kennedy."

Or even Lawford, for that matter.

Victoria Francis Lawford

(b. November 4, 1958)

MIMING MUMMY

Mummy was always doing things with us—taking us to museums and concerts and art shows and stuff. I'd want my children to have the same kind of life I had. I never thought about it until recently, but it has become clear to me that my mother was there for us all the time. We were her life's work.
—VICTORIA LAWFORD, in *Growing Up Kennedy*

Victoria Lawford made the above remarks *before* she was married and had children, and it reveals that as she grew into adulthood, she began to give more thought to the value of being an involved mother and to recognize that parenting can, indeed, be a "life's work." Her mother Pat had instilled in all her children the importance of family and raising children properly.

Victoria Francis Lawford's name has an interesting pedigree. On November 4, 1958, the day she was born, her uncle Jack Kennedy had just been reelected to a second term as a United States senator. In honor of this auspicious event, Pat and Peter Lawford named their new daughter "Victoria" to celebrate her uncle Jack's victory.

Victoria's middle name of "Francis" was also a tribute of sorts, this time to Francis Albert (Frank) Sinatra, one of Peter Lawford's close friends and fellow "Rat Pack" member. Peter and Pat were bold in using "Francis": they did not opt for the more appropriate feminine spelling of "Frances," instead sticking with the masculine spelling.

When Victoria was born, the Lawfords were busy people. Pat and Peter were in the middle of negotiations to buy the rights to the script for a movie called *Ocean's Eleven*, a "caper" film about five friends who plan on robbing five Las Vegas casinos at the same time. The film was ultimately made and released in 1960, starring Peter Lawford's fellow "Rat Pack" cohorts, Frank Sinatra, Sammy Davis Jr., and Dean Martin.

As they had done with son Christopher, Peter and Pat once again delegated most of the care of their newborn to a nursemaid as soon as Victoria was brought home from the hospital. Eleven days later, they signed the *Ocean's Eleven* deal, securing the rights to the screenplay for ten thousand dollars.

Following Pat and Peter's divorce in the mid-sixties, Pat took over raising their children on the East Coast. Victoria tried to maintain contact with her distant and apparently indifferent father, and at one point, when she was in her teens, wrote him a letter in which she told him, "I've never really had a chance to sit down and talk to you as daughter to father, but I guess I feel just as close to you as if I had."

Victoria received a wonderful education, attending the Convent of the Sacred Heart with cousin Caroline and sister Sydney, and she even spent two years in France studying at the Lycée Français, graduating from there in 1976. She later graduated from Mt. Vernon College in 1980, and then set her sights on finding a job.

It was Victoria's job-hunting ordeal that probably convinced her that coming from a famous family did not always guarantee a warm welcome into the enclaves of the business world. Reportedly, Victoria Lawford spent a year and a half looking for a job. She was bright, talented, attractive, and ambitious, and yet, she couldn't get hired. Why? Because none of the people who interviewed her could believe that a Kennedy grandchild could seriously be in need of a job.

She finally acquired a position working for a small cable TV outlet that covered local politics and the like. She apparently had a long-term goal of a high-profile, on-camera job, but abandoned those plans after marrying and having children.

One job Victoria had that she did embrace and give her all to, though, was that of TV coordinator for Very Special Arts, a nonprofit affiliate of the JFK Center for the Performing Arts. This group develops programs for the disabled, and Victoria played an active role in its operation. Victoria's cousin Kara, with whom she is very close, also served in a similar capacity with Very Special Arts before making the same choice to be a stay-at-home mom.

Victoria's uncles Ted and Bobby made a great impression on her when she was growing up and she recalls her uncle Ted especially taking a great interest in what was going on in her life and talking to her about things that were bothering her. She worked in Ted's 1980 campaign, shyly asking people, "Would you think about voting for my Uncle Ted?"

Victoria married attorney Robert Pender in 1987, and they have three children—Alexandra, Caroline, and Victoria. The Penders live in Washington, DC, and keep a low profile, with Victoria rarely, if ever, commenting publicly on the triumphs and tribulations of her many Kennedy cousins.

Robin Elizabeth Lawford

(b. July 2, 1961)

THE SCIENTIST

Your entrance is timely, as we need a new left end.
—PRESIDENT JOHN F. KENNEDY, in a note to his new niece
Robin Lawford, shortly after her birth.

Robin Elizabeth Lawford, the youngest child of Patricia Kennedy and Peter Lawford, holds a special distinction among the Kennedy third generation.

Of the twenty-seven surviving grandchildren of Rose and Joe Kennedy, there are politicians and lawyers galore, as well as writers, businessmen, people in the media, homemakers, and even an actor; but there is only one scientist, and that is Robin Lawford, the marine biologist. Marine biology might be considered an unexpected career choice for one of the Kennedy kin, and yet it *is* a vocation that makes sense for someone from a family known for its social and environmental activism.

The field of marine biology today is concerned with the oceans and its inhabitants, and as a practicing marine biologist, Robin's focus is protection and preservation of the seas and the many species that inhabit it, some of which are on the verge of extinction. So perhaps, Robin's career path is not that unexpected after all.

Robin weighed five and one half pounds at birth and after her mother Pat had gotten a good look at her, she wrote to her parents, who were then off on a holiday on the French Riviera, "Red hair and the longest fingers I've ever seen. So maybe she'll have Dad's brains, too!"

A week after she was born, Robin was baptized at St. Monica's Church. Her uncle Bobby Kennedy was her godfather, and Frank Sinatra and other Hollywood luminaries attended the celebration. Shortly after her christening, when Robin was barely a month old, her parents Pat and Peter went off on a Mediterranean cruise, leaving the newborn with a nanny and other staff.

Shortly after the Lawfords had left on their cruise, little Robin had a serious medical crisis. The vacationing parents received a telegram on the ship telling them that Robin had been rushed to the hospital because she wouldn't stop choking. With treatment, she came out of the choking spell and was sent home. Pat and Peter were assured that she was fine and they decided to continue their trip.

Three days later, however, Robin had to be readmitted to the hospital, this time with an intestinal blockage known as pyloric stenosis. This condition, which most commonly occurs in newborn males between the fourth and sixth week of life, is normally not present at birth. Within the first few weeks of life, however, a muscular obstruction forms that almost completely blocks off the infant's gastrointestinal tract. Robin's earlier choking incident was likely related to this obstruction, since vomiting and inability to digest food is a common symptom of this life-threatening condition.

As soon as Pat and Peter were informed of Robin's rehospitalization, they decided to return home immediately. At Heathrow Airport in London, the worried parents were told that Robin needed immediate surgery and they granted consent through the White House physician, Dr. Janet Travell. Upon leaving the private lounge where they had been discussing Robin's surgery, Pat and Peter were faced with a swarm of reporters clamoring for a statement. "My baby's going to have an operation in five or six hours," Pat said, near tears, and then got on the plane to return to Los Angeles.

The anxious parents were given word on the plane that the surgery had gone well and that Robin was expected to completely recover. "I guess you can realize how worried Pat and I were," Peter Lawford told the assembled press when their plane landed in Los Angeles. "[W]e are pleased and happy that Robin is all right."

Peter and Pat Lawford took a lot of heat from the media for their decision to leave a month-old baby and go on a cruise. The high-profile couple never responded to the criticism.

Robin graduated from the Unis School in 1980 and went on to Marymount College. She was involved with the Kennedy Child Study Center in New York City for a time, and also worked as a stage manager in several Off-Off Broadway theatrical productions when she was in her late twenties.

Robin spent a couple of years in Paris with her mother and her sister Victoria, and when she returned, devoted herself to attaining her marine biology degree. Today, Robin is still single. She tends to keep a low profile, but does show up at many of the fundraising events in which her family is involved. Considering her career path and interests, it is unlikely that Robin Lawford has a calling for either of the two vocations of her family, politics or journalism.

Sometimes the Kennedy grandchildren do unexpected things, and the day may come where we see the scientist daughter of a world-famous actor get more involved in the political world. But until then, the seas and their denizens are the main concerns of Robin Lawford.

The Children of
Ethel Skakel and
Robert F. Kennedy

Kathleen Hartington Kennedy
(b. July 4, 1951)

THE STRANDS THAT FORM HER

I want to live so that each day is crucial, each day really important, so I will have lived each moment the best way I can, even if tomorrow isn't there.
  —KATHLEEN KENNEDY TOWNSEND

In 1968, sixteen-year-old Kathleen Kennedy was working on an Indian reservation in Globe, Arizona, teaching Navaho children how to read and speak English.

This admirable effort on her part was prompted by a visit to another Indian reservation a couple of years earlier during a delay in a rafting trip down the Colorado River. This previous visit had opened Kathleen's eyes and thrown into stark contrast the disparity between the life of privilege and comfort she lived as a Kennedy and the often difficult and challenging lives the poor in this country were forced to lead. So, two summers later, Kathleen decided to try and help by spending some time teaching the Native American children.

But Kathleen Kennedy was not just another high schooler filling up a summer vacation with an exotic sabbatical, motivated more by the novelty of the trip than by selflessness and a sense of duty. Kathleen was Robert F. Kennedy's daughter, and as such, she realized that she had an obligation to help, and that being who she was, she could truly do some good for these people.

In *Growing Up Kennedy*, Kathleen frankly admitted that, "Many privileges go with the name." She also thoughtfully commented, "Basically, there are two aspects to being a Kennedy. The first is that the family has been given a lot and should give a lot in return. The second is that the Kennedys are famous. Without Daddy, the focus tended more to the second."

But Kathleen, even at an early age, was determined to use her famous name to help. This commitment to service was what brought her to the reservation, and once she was there, she saw one roadblock to the Navahos making any kind of significant progress: the long road that led to their reservation was unpaved and difficult to travel. Recognizing how important it was for the reservation to be more accessible, Kathleen sprang into action. She recounted what happened next for Kennedy biographers Harrison Rainie and John Quinn: "So I called Mummy and told her, and I think she called the Secretary of the Interior and the road was eventually paved."

To Kathleen, the end result of the road being paved was the tangible result of effective and proper use of her name and connections. The fact that a teenage girl could spur the United States Secretary of the Interior into action speaks volumes about the clout the Kennedy name wielded—and continues to wield in twentieth century America. It also illustrates what motivates Kathleen, the Kennedy daughter whom the family holds in especially high regard.

Kathleen Hartington Kennedy Townsend is one of the two children of Robert and Ethel Kennedy who were born on the Fourth of July. The other is her brother Chris. Kathleen, however, now has one of the most notable political jobs of all the members of the younger generation of Kennedys: she has been the lieutenant governor of Maryland since 1994.

There have been several "firsts" in the life of Robert and Ethel Kennedy's oldest child. Kathleen, named for RFK's sister, Kathleen "Kick" Kennedy, was the first of the eleven children born to the senator and his wife. Kathleen was also the first of the third-generation of Kennedys to marry. In 1973, she wed teacher and writer David Townsend. At one point in the early years of her marriage, her grandmother Rose wrote Kathleen a note telling her how pleased she was knowing her eldest grandchild had a strong and happy marriage. In 1977, Kathleen and her husband David gave birth to Meaghan Ann, the first of the *fourth* generation of Kennedys and the first great-grandchild of Joe and Rose Kennedy. And in 1986, Kathleen, at the age of thirty-four, declared her candidacy for a congressional seat in the House of Representatives from Maryland, her husband's home state—the first Kennedy woman ever to run for public office.

That same year, Kathleen—who chose to run as "Kathleen Townsend" and not use the Kennedy name on campaign signs—lost the election; again, a first: She was the first Kennedy *ever* to lose a general election.

As the first of the younger generation of Kennedys, Kathleen's birth was significant to the family and to the country.

Kathleen was baptized by none other than the renowned cleric Cardinal Richard Cushing, and her godfather was a Trappist monk named Danny Walsh. Walsh was the cleric who had converted the legendary German philosopher and writer Thomas Mann (*Buddenbrooks, Death in Venice, The Magic Mountain*) to Roman Catholicism.

As a child, Kathleen was full of energy and often acted as a surrogate mother to her younger siblings; the youngest of the ten already born at the time of RFK's assassination—

Douglas—was only a year old when his father was killed. Rory was born after RFK's death. We now know that Kathleen's mother, Ethel Kennedy, was overwhelmed by the murder and loss of her husband, and the subsequent lone responsibility of properly raising their eleven children. As an adolescent, Kathleen assumed some of that burden.

Like many girls born into money, Kathleen became involved with horses and equestrian sports as a child, and in *The Other Mrs. Kennedy,* author Jerry Oppenheimer recounts one particularly dramatic episode that occurred during her riding career.

When Kathleen was fourteen, she won four blue ribbons for excellence at a horse show. In August 1965, during a competition at Sea Flash Farms in West Barnstable, Massachusetts, Kathleen's horse—Attorney General, named, of course, in honor of her father—tripped during a jump, throwing Kathleen through the air. She landed hard enough to be knocked unconscious. Kathleen was rushed to Cape Cod Hospital where an examination indicated internal bleeding and possible kidney damage.

Kathleen's family was out sailing at the time of the accident. They were out on the boat, *The Neris,* in rough seas, and when the Coast Guard found them and used a bullhorn to give them the news that Kathleen had been hurt. RFK leaped overboard and swam to the Coast Guard cutter, such was his impatience to get to the hospital.

Kathleen ended up with a mild concussion, a contusion of the bladder, and internal bleeding. Her uncle Ted Kennedy had two doctors flown in from Boston for consultation. Kathleen recovered. This was not just another riding accident, though, and, again, the Kennedy name worked its magic.

During her recuperation, Kathleen received a huge bowl of yellow Texas roses from President Lyndon Johnson, accompanied by a personal note in which he wrote, "It's no fun to part company with a horse, especially in mid-air, and I speak from experience." LBJ then quoted the song "Pick Yourself Up" from the 1936 movie *Swing Time* ("Pick yourself up, brush yourself off, and start all over again"), assuring her that she was just the girl to not let something like this dampen her interest in riding.

Since the Kennedys as a family were devoutly Roman Catholic, when she was a child, Kathleen attended the Stone Ridge Country Day School of the Sacred Heart in Bethesda, Maryland, where she was given a strict Catholic education. Kathleen's friend Anne Coffey, in *The Kennedy Women*, remembered that, "Kathleen arrived kicking and screaming, throwing the worst temper tantrum I've ever seen" (p. 490). Kathleen eventually settled in at the school, but soon found other difficulties with Stone Ridge, these of a more philosophical nature.

Kathleen's time at the school marked the beginning of her struggle with Catholicism's strict doctrines, particularly with regard to gender. Even at an early age she embraced feminist ideals and has been quoted as calling the Catholic church's treatment of women "suffocating."

Classmates of Kathleen's from this period remember her always arguing in religion class, and eventually, she felt she had to separate herself from Stone Ridge and the inflexible Roman Catholic point of view the school espoused, a perspective Kathleen once described as "chauvinistic." In her early teens, Kathleen stopped attending Mass and transferred to the Putney School in Vermont, a place she described as "full of radicals," and an educational institution she hoped would liberate her from what she had come to see as repressive views of Catholicism.

At Putney, Kathleen studied side by side with children from all social and economic classes. She cultivated her interest in social service while at Putney and was accepted at Radcliffe College upon graduation. It has been suggested in many Kennedy family biographies that Kathleen felt obligated to attend Radcliffe because it was the female counterpart to Harvard, the alma mater of her father, uncles, and grandfather. Whether she felt this way or not, she did attend and ultimately graduated cum laude from the august institution.

After a post-high-school summer sabbatical in Alaska, where she worked in a day care center, Kathleen began Radcliffe. During her time there, she spent one semester abroad, living and studying in Florence, Italy, where she resided with an Italian mechanic and his family. While living in Italy, Kathleen also became a vegetarian, learned to speak Italian, and mastered the art of making pottery. Her skill as a potter later prompted her bridesmaids to give her a rather unique wedding gift: they all chipped in and brought Kathleen her own potter's wheel.

At Radcliffe, Kathleen met her future husband, David Townsend, a teacher who was four years older than her and whose doctoral thesis at Harvard had been on American visionary poetry. After a one-year courtship, David and Kathleen were married on November 17, 1973 at Holy Trinity Church in Georgetown. Kathleen was twenty-two and a senior at Radcliffe, and the two lovers recited poetry to each other at the ceremony. The story of Kathleen's wedding is yet another example of how "nonordinary" life can be when you are part of a family of consequence.

Kathleen was going through her "flower child" stage at the time of her wedding. She wore flowers in her hair and her husband-to-be wore a somewhat longish beard. David also made their wedding rings by hand, and if Kathleen was anyone else, she probably would have had their reception in a pasture and gone barefoot for the ceremony.

However, Kathleen could not escape the Kennedy name, and thus, the day was notable for the odd blending of a "peace and love" motif with the inescapable aura that always accompanied the presence of some of the political and cultural elite of the day. Kathleen's wedding guests included writer Art

Buchwald, former astronaut and senator John Glenn, Democratic presidential candidate George McGovern, actress Angie Dickinson, and others of their ilk. Kathleen wore an expensive Oleg Cassini gown, and celebrated singer Andy Williams performed "Ave Maria" and "Panis Angelicus." It was most decidedly not an ordinary wedding.

Kathleen's wedding day also included high drama. November 17 was the same day that her cousin Ted Kennedy Jr. (Senator Edward Kennedy's son) was having his cancerous right leg amputated, with the surgery taking place at Georgetown University Hospital a mere one hour before Kathleen and David's ceremony. Through one of those weird concatenations of scheduling everyone occasionally experiences, Kathleen's wedding and Ted's surgery had both been booked for the same day, and neither could be changed. Of course Kathleen would have understood if Uncle Ted couldn't make the wedding because he wanted to be with his son. After all, her Aunt Jackie declined attending. But Uncle Ted was giving the bride away and, thus, *had* to be there.

Sure enough, Teddy came through. The senator wore his tuxedo to the hospital, made sure the surgery on his son went smoothly, and then rushed to the church where he proudly walked his brother's daughter down the aisle. Thanks to the willing participation of Kathleen's substantial clan, the rest of the wedding went off without a hitch: her sisters Courtney and Kerry, and her cousin Caroline served as bridesmaids; no less than six Kennedy brothers served as ushers. Kathleen's youngest siblings, four-year-old Rory and six-year-old Douglas, served as the ring-bearers.

After they were married, Kathleen and David remained in Cambridge, Massachusetts, while Kathleen finished her senior year at Radcliffe. After graduation, they moved to Santa Fe, New Mexico, where they lived a somewhat spartan and rustic life. David taught school while Kathleen took a job with the Human Rights Commission. Kathleen eventually enrolled at the University of New Mexico, where she pursued a law degree while working part-time at a Santa Fe newspaper.

Kathleen and David's first child, Meaghan Ann Kennedy, was born on November 8, 1977. With David's help, Kathleen gave birth to Meaghan at home, and after the delivery, they stored Meaghan's placenta in their refrigerator.

During one of her visits to the happy couple in New Mexico, Kathleen's mother, Ethel Kennedy, was shocked to find an afterbirth in their refrigerator and asked them why they were saving it. They explained that they planned on performing an ancient ritualistic tradition they had heard about in which new parents buried their child's placenta in the ground and then planted a tree above it. Obviously, they had not gotten around to actually executing the ritual yet, so new grandmother Ethel, understandably eager to get little Meaghan's placenta out of the refrigerator, dug a hole, buried the vascular organ, and planted the tree herself.

Two years later, in September 1979, David and Kathleen's second daughter, Maeve Fahey, was born in their new home in New Haven, Connecticut. Two years after her birth, in 1981, the family moved to Boston, where Kathleen managed her uncle Ted's 1982 senatorial reelection campaign. She then went to work as a policy analyst for Governor Michael Dukakis' Office of Human Resources, while David stayed at home, taking care of their girls and writing a novel.

In 1984, these nomads moved yet again, this time to Baltimore in David's home state of Maryland, where David took a teaching job at St. John's College in Annapolis. They had their third daughter in 1984, Rose Katherine—named for her grandmother—and that same year, Kathleen created the Robert F. Kennedy Human Rights Award in her father's memory. The first recipient of the award was the Co-Madres, the Committee of Mothers and Relatives of Political Prisoners, Disappeared and Murdered of El Salvador.

On February 1, 1986, Kathleen declared her candidacy for

the House of Representatives in Maryland's Second District, becoming, as we have already noted, the first Kennedy woman to ever run for elective office. Years later, talking about her surprising plunge into the "family business," Kathleen said, "It was never expected that I would go into politics . . . It was not even dreamed about, talked about, thought of. It wasn't in the realm of possibility."

Unconcerned about her appearance, Kathleen campaigned diligently, but with a short hair style, drab business suits, and enormous glasses, she looked more like a stuffy college professor than a vibrant young woman who could instigate political change and improve people's lives. Campaigning as *Kathleen Townsend*, she probably believed that her message and her concern for the issues, as well as her pro-choice position, were enough to get her elected. There seemed to be a reluctance on Kathleen's part to trade on the venerable Kennedy name, no matter what benefits such exploitation might have yielded.

Even though she tried to develop a more effective speaking voice and dramatic presence, Kathleen did not remind people of her father. Laurence Leamer, writing in *The Kennedy Women*, makes the point that, "Those who came seeking resonances of her father and uncle usually came away disappointed." Kathleen believes she knocked on over ten thousand doors during her inaugural campaign, but to no avail. She lost the election.

Kathleen gave birth to her and David's fourth daughter, Kerry, in 1992, and did not run for office again until 1994. That year, she resigned her position as deputy assistant attorney general for the Clinton Justice Department in order to run for lieutenant governor of Maryland. This time she ran as Kathleen Kennedy Townsend and won handily. During the campaign she told *People* magazine, "My family has been terrific. My favorite part is campaigning with the children. I call them the feminist cooperative."

Now in her fourth year of her term as lieutenant governor,

Kathleen continues to write essays and articles for a range of periodicals, including *The Washington Monthly*. In her most recent article for that journal, her June 1996 essay, "Don't Be An *Idios:* The Case for Participation in Public Life," Kathleen continues to stress her seminal theme, that of citizen involvement in government:

> The challenge now is to return to the original Jeffersonian ideal, in which everybody—not just the experts, not just the wealthy—can participate in government. For too long, Republicans have simply knocked national government and looked only to voluntary local solutions. For too long, Democrats have thought that the national government had to solve every problem on its own, meanwhile forgetting the need for local participation. But clearly we need both. If we really hope to restore a sense of the rewards of citizenship, we have to stop treating people like customers and start treating them like Americans.

Two months prior to this *Washington Monthly* article, Kathleen published a powerfully written piece in the April 1996 issue of *Ladies Home Journal*, "No More Name-Calling," in which she cogently and passionately decried the pervasive ugliness of tone and rhetoric permeating the political process today. Here, she deftly uses her own family history to make her point:

> I am not a great believer that out of tragedy comes good. There is no doubt that our nation would be a better place if Abraham Lincoln; Martin Luther King, Jr.; my uncle, John F. Kennedy; and my father, Robert Kennedy, had not been killed. Through their work and their example, these men united people who once were separate; they helped disparate groups see and

understand each other. We are a lesser country for their deaths.

When I was growing up, I was taught that politics was a noble calling and the democratic process was something to be treated with respect. . . . Today, the issues seem to have taken a backseat to name-calling and demonizing.

Kathleen's concern for social issues and her diligent efforts to improve conditions in the areas of housing, education, and crime, emanate from her strong religious grounding in Catholicism; a faith that she felt driven to challenge in her early years, but which she now wholeheartedly embraces. She has stated that the issues that motivate her were defined for her by the beliefs of Catholicism, a system of influences she has described as "the strands that form you."

These moral mandates—which she obviously views as separate from the rules and regulations of the Catholic faith—molded Kathleen, and continue to serve as ethical guideposts for her as she works as the lieutenant governor of Maryland. These "strands" are what makes her who she is: as she has said, "It's really hard to separate them."

Joseph Patrick Kennedy II
(b. September 24, 1952)

WEARING HIS FATHER'S SUITS

I like clinging to the side of a mountain, sailing across the ocean, or fighting an angry bull. Some people don't like the feeling. I happen to love it. These are exciting things. They give a person a feeling of accomplishment — of self-confidence.
— Joe Kennedy II

One night, Joseph Patrick Kennedy II was working on a speech for his uncle Ted's 1976 reelection campaign. Joe decided that the speech really needed a great joke to start things off and endear Uncle Ted to his listeners, but he didn't feel up to the task of crafting a really terrific gag.

Joe, however, is one of the august Kennedy clan, and, as we have seen over the years, the Kennedys have myriad resources unavailable to commoners. So even though it was close to midnight, Joe picked up the phone and called someone who had had some experience writing jokes and who he knew could help him. Joe called Woody Allen, explained his plight, and the Woodman happily provided Joe with a brilliantly pithy witticism that went over quite well with Ted's supporters the following day.

❊   ❊   ❊

Two days after his brother Jack was assassinated, Robert F. Kennedy wrote a letter to his oldest son, Joseph Patrick.

"You are the oldest of all the male grandchildren," RFK wrote. "You have a special and particular responsibility now which I know you will fulfill. Remember all the things that Jack started—be kind to others that are less fortunate than we—and love our country."

This blatant acknowledgment of Joe's "legacy" was apparently not something he warmly embraced when he was young. Even later, when he was running for Congress in Boston, he publicly rejected the notion of a "Kennedy legacy." "That's a crock of baloney," he told a reporter while out campaigning. "I don't believe there's any kind of mantle. What there are, are certain assets I can use for positive goals . . . but I'm not carrying around all that baggage."

Joe has also gone on record, saying that he believes there was a conspiracy surrounding the assassination of JFK. He has stated that he believes the same people were responsible for his own father's death.

As has often been noted, Joe II was named for two men: his grandfather, Joe, the patriarch of the Kennedy family, and his uncle Joe, a fighter pilot who was killed at the age of twenty-nine during World War II.

In his early years, Joe embodied many of the best and worst traits of the men in his family. His childhood was troubled with such academic difficulties that some friends and family members feared he was dyslexic. He earned his high school diploma from the somewhat less-demanding Manter Hall Tutoring School in Cambridge, Massachusetts, after transferring out of several other schools—Our Lady of Victory School, Georgetown Preparatory School, and Milton Academy.

According to the authors of *Growing Up Kennedy*, a com-

mon, if clandestinely-asked, question in the Kennedy family
when Joe was growing up was, "What's the matter with
Joe?" When asked later whether or not he had a learning
disability as a child, Joe has stated, "I really don't know."

At Milton Academy, Joe had to endure mental and physical torments because of his name. According to Milton class-
mate and Joe's "Big Brother" Tim Draydock, upperclassmen
frequently tested Joe because they "wanted to see how much
he could take." They short-sheeted his bed and deliberately
vomited on his pillow. Girls would pretend to be interested
in Joe just so they could get some kind of note from him—
in the hopes that someday his signature would be worth
something.

Joe definitely had his moments. After his father's death,
a remarkably poised and dignified sixteen-year-old Joe
walked up and down the aisle of the train which carried the
body of his slain father, shaking everyone's hand and telling
them, "I'm Joe Kennedy. Thank you for coming." This ma-
ture and apparently unexpected performance by Joe moved
his mother Ethel to tell friends that she thought Joe had
"it"—"it" being, of course, that irresistible Kennedy charm
that not all members of the family are lucky enough to pos-
sess. His appreciative stroll through the train was broadcast
on network TV, and it was the beginning of a journey that
would lead to Joe being elected to the congressional seat once
held by his uncle Jack.

After his father's assassination, all eyes looked to Joe to
assume the responsibilities of being "the man of the house."
At Hickory Hill, Joe was granted the privilege of sitting in
his father's seat at the head of the table during meals. In the
early seventies, while Joe was working as a volunteer at the
Daniel Marr Boys Center in Boston, he even wore his father's
suits. But at the time of RFK's death, Joe lacked the emotional maturity everyone seemed to expect and demand from
him.

Joe may have been what *Current Biography* described as "the heir to the mantle of the patrilineal Kennedy family political dynasty," but he was still only sixteen years old, and he did not know how to handle this new burden. In an outburst of arrogance, Joe once slapped his sister Kerry in the face for talking too loudly. Newly crowned "head of the family" or not, his mother Ethel refused to tolerate such behavior, and she punished him the way she would one of his younger siblings: she made him walk up and down a flight of stairs one hundred times.

Risk, danger, and high drama seem to have been frequent visitors to Joe's life during his adolescence. In the summer of 1968, shortly after his father's death, Joe traveled to Spain with his uncle Ted. Capitulating to the dares and taunts of the photographers and reporters following him, Joe recklessly agreed to fight a bull—with absolutely no training whatsoever. Of course, Joe wound up injured, and pictures of his bloody face were on the front page of countless newspapers and broadcast on news shows all over the world. This incident made Joe come across as just one more reckless, spoiled Kennedy, and it did nothing to enhance his image or convince the world that he was up to the task of walking in his father's shoes.

At the age of eighteen, Joe helped out with his uncle Ted's 1970 campaign and got his first taste of the machinations of American politics. In 1971, Joe worked on an ABC documentary in Kenya called *American Sportsman* and, during filming, a raging antelope attacked the horse Joe was riding. Joe escaped without injury, though he did reportedly contract malaria during the trip. In 1972, Joe traveled to Bangladesh with his mother Ethel and his uncle Ted. Only twenty at the time, Joe made the bold decision to buy a motorcycle and ride through the central states of India by himself rather than return home with his family. Even though his motorcycle trip was relatively uneventful, his return flight home was anything but. Joe's Lufthansa flight was hijacked by five Palestinian terrorists who rigged the plane with powerful explosives. Joe and the other passengers were held hostage for eighteen hours before being released. Of this ordeal, Joe later said, "It wasn't the worst moment of my life. I've been scared before, but it never lasted as long." After his hijacking ordeal, Joe worked for a time for the Robert F. Kennedy Memorial Organization. He also visited Indian reservations in San Diego County, worked for the George McGovern campaign, and met with migrant farm workers in Jackson, Mississippi.

Joe was twenty-one in the summer of 1973. One day, while out driving with a bunch of friends and his brother, David, Joe overturned his Jeep, seriously injuring David and his friend Pamela Kelley, who was left paralyzed from the waist down. Joe was found guilty of negligent driving and given a stern lecture by Nantucket Judge C. George Anastos, who told him, "I would hope you would use your illustrious name as an example that could be an asset to the young people of your age instead of becoming involved in cases that bring you in to court." The judge also told Joe, "I knew your father in Washington. We did not always agree on matters, but he was a fine man. You have a fine mother."

The Kennedy family ultimately settled with Pam Kelley for one million dollars, set up in a trust that provides lifetime care for her and assures she will never have to worry about an income.

This accident had other dire repercussions: Joe's younger brother David was also injured in the crash and became addicted to drugs after being given prescription narcotics for pain in the hospital.

The accident was one of the factors contributing to the maturing of Joe Kennedy II, a process helped along by a heart-to-heart with his "surrogate father," Ted Kennedy, following the tragedy.

After brief sojourns at the Massachusetts Institute of

Technology and the University of California at Berkeley, Joe graduated in 1976 from the University of Massachusetts with a degree in legal services. He managed his uncle Ted's 1976 senatorial reelection campaign and was involved in the building and dedication of the John F. Kennedy Memorial Library, an institution built to honor both JFK and RFK.

In June 1979, Joe gave a speech at the dedication of the library, but this wasn't just an ordinary speech. That day, Joe "took no prisoners," so to speak, and he left the sensibilities of many of those who were present metaphorically bloody and beaten.

Joe was incensed, first of all, that the one-hour biographical video presentation scheduled to be shown that day included forty-five minutes of material about JFK and only fifteen minutes about his father. He also used the forum he was given that day to condemn big-profit oil companies and to criticize President Jimmy Carter's energy policies. This would have been nothing more than a passionate issues-oriented speech except for a couple of factors that elevated it into the realm of painful embarrassment for those who were there that day. First of all, President Jimmy Carter was at the dedication ceremony that day and could not avoid the obvious attack on his policies. Senator Ted Kennedy, who was planning on challenging Carter in that fall's Democratic primary, was also there, leaving an impression that Joe was blatantly campaigning for Ted by denigrating Carter in front of the assembled media. Ted, however, had had no idea what Joe was going to talk about that day and uncomfortably shifted in his seat during Joe's tirade. Joe continued to hammer home his points, however, even bringing to bear the term "moral courage," a favorite buzzword and call to arms of his late father.

The members of the younger generation of Kennedys who heard Joe that day were ecstatic. Joe's cousins all cheered him following his speech, and many thought they had witnessed something momentous—that they had been present at the birth of the next wearer of the Kennedy political crown. Ted Kennedy has been quoted as saying that Joe's speech was "the high point of the day," but this may have been a somewhat ineffectual attempt to diffuse a volatile moment and put a positive spin on something that Ted probably wished never happened.

Joe's attack on the oil companies that day resulted in what may be his greatest achievement. In the midst of the 1979 oil crisis, Joe formed the nonprofit Citizens Energy Corporation, an organization that would use its profit to lower the price of oil it would sell to poor families. Joe's company slogan was, "No One Should Be Left Out in the Cold. Phone Joe Kennedy."

Through careful budgeting, smart deal-making, and a philanthropic vision and mission statement, Joe was able to sell heating oil to Boston's poor at 57¢ a gallon—when the prevailing retail price was 82¢ a gallon. He also started lending money to selected landlords who were willing to make their rental units more energy efficient. He quickly branched out from just selling home heating oil into alternative energy programs involving foreign countries. His first project, completed in September 1981, installed a solar hot water heating system in a hospital in Montego Bay, Jamaica.

Joe Kennedy II, who gave himself a salary of only $50,000 a year from the CEC, succeeded in creating something no one believed was viable and everyone said was ultimately impossible: Joe Kennedy created the world's first *charitable* oil company.

In 1986, Joe decided to run for JFK's Eighth Congressional District seat in his home state of Massachusetts. There were several candidates all vying for the same seat, including President Franklin D. Roosevelt's grandson James Roosevelt Jr. and black leader Melvin King.

Joe spent $1.5 million on his campaign and handily won

the primary and the general election. The Kennedy politicians had always thrown big money at their campaigns, and Joe was apparently no different, generating accusations that he had bought the election. Those charges notwithstanding, Joe has been reelected twice since his initial election, and he has a strong following among all strata of his district's voters.

Aside from his highly public political career and acclaimed business endeavors, Joe's private life has been relatively sedate, except perhaps for the expected Kennedyesque "womanizing" when he was younger.

In 1974, Joe met his first wife, Sheila Rauch, at a party in Hyannis Port. She was a sharp-minded Harvard grad student and they hit it off immediately. They were married in June 1979 and had twin boys, Joe II and Matthew in 1981. At his wedding reception, Joe's brother Bobby toasted the happy couple: "Sheila, you are now going to be a roommate of Joe's. I used to be a roommate and I understand what it will be like for you. Not good. My roommate once killed my turtles for no reason."

Joe and Sheila's marriage ended in 1990 when they separated, and Joe began a romantic relationship with his assistant Beth Kelly. He married Beth in 1993 after a public embarrassment concerning his and Sheila's divorce. Joe tried to get his marriage to Sheila annulled so that he could marry Beth in a Catholic ceremony—but he didn't bother to tell Sheila that he was pursuing an annulment. "He didn't come to me," Sheila told the newspaper the *Boston Globe* after their separation. "He had the Catholic Church send me a notice in the mail. It was devastating, but subtlety's never been one of Joe's strong points." Sheila said she threw up after reading the letter. She was incensed at Joe's actions and publicly made it clear that she would not sit still for it: "I will continue to defend the bond that brought my children into the world," she said. "I'm not going to lie in front of God so Joe can have a big Catholic wedding."

After a time, Joe reached the point where he obviously had no confidence in ever getting an annulment when one of the parties was so adamantly opposed to it, and so, on October 23, 1993, Joe wed Beth Kelly in the foyer of his home in Brighton, Massachusetts. A justice of the peace performed the ceremony and there were 140 guests in attendance. Exiled Haitian President Jean Bertrand Aristide read from the scriptures during the ceremony, and the buffet included the unusual offering of Triscuit crackers topped with peanut butter and bacon bits, a favorite snack of the happy couple.

In the spring of 1997, Sheila Rauch Kennedy's book about her and Joe's breakup was published by Pantheon Books. It was titled *Shattered Faith: A Woman's Struggle to Stop the Catholic Church from Annulling Her Marriage* and recounted the story of their divorce and her rage at Joe's attempt to get their marriage annulled. *The Boston Herald* ran an excerpt from the book and some speculated that the book's release was timed to coincide with the period in which Joe would be making up his mind whether or not to run for the Massachusetts governor's office.

In March 1997, Joe Kennedy issued a statement in which he said he did not know if the book's release would influence his political future. "People will have to make their own decisions," he told reporters. Of the book itself, Joe said, "This is a very personal matter. I love my family very much. I understand Sheila's feelings and respect her right to express them."

In *Shattered Faith*, Sheila pulled no punches. "My former husband," she wrote, "was powerful and popular. I was, as he so often reminded me, a nobody; and nobody in his town would be on my side." She also wrote, "I had never faced the truth that by the end of our marriage I had simply become afraid of him."

The annulment of Joe and Sheila's marriage was granted in October 1996. At the time her book was published, Sheila was appealing to the Rota—the Roman Catholic church court—to reverse their decision and invalidate the annulment. Of the annulment, which was granted based on a "lack of due discretion," Sheila wrote, "In other words, at the time of our marriage, Joe had suffered from a lack of due discretion of such magnitude that he was incapable of marriage, and therefore our union had never been valid."

A New York newspaper ran a column about the book and titled the article, "Hell Hath No Fury Dept."

Until early 1998, Joe was a thrice-elected representative from the Commonwealth of Massachusetts. As noted, there was ongoing speculation that he had his eyes set on the 1998 Massachusetts governor's race, but his brother Michael's death on New Year's Eve 1997 impelled him to quit politics completely and to return to running the Citizen's Energy Corporation full-time.

In early 1997, Joe was at odds with his uncle Ted and his cousin, Rhode Island Representative Patrick Kennedy (Ted's son), over the merits of a constitutional amendment to require a balanced federal budget. Ted described the proposed amendment as "a turkey," while Joe believed the amendment was needed to prevent Congress from overspending. But Uncle Ted had the last word in this good-natured battle: "It's two Kennedys against one," Ted told the press.

Joe may have been outnumbered in that fight, but his being in it at all is a sign of how much he has matured since his family and the public first looked to him as a replacement for his father. In the seventies he physically wore his father's suits. Today it is clear that he worked hard to assume his father's mantle of political strength and responsibility.

Robert "Bobby" Francis Kennedy Jr.

(b. January 17, 1954)

KEEPING THE DEMONS AWAY

Life for him was an adventure, perilous indeed, but men are not made for safe havens.
—EDITH HAMILTON's description of Aeschylus that RFK hung in the master bedroom at Hickory Hill.

Mother Teresa does not demand that we succeed. She demands that we try.
—BOBBY JR.

The teenage boy with the dark hair sits cross-legged on the floor in front of a blazing fireplace. Slowly, deliberately, he tears pages from that day's *Washington Post* and feeds them into the fire. He waits until each burning page is nothing but a thin shell of black ash before he touches the corner of the next page to the flames. He continues burning the pages of the newspaper for over half an hour until there is nothing left in his ink-stained hands to burn. He then continues to sit there on the floor, Indian-style, staring into the fire.

As the yellow and orange blaze dances before his eyes, the smiling face of his father suddenly appears in the flames, and then just as quickly transforms into the scorched, stone face of a man lying on his back on a bed of blood on the floor of a hotel kitchen.

Days later, Bobby Kennedy Jr. will serve as a pallbearer at his father's funeral. He will stand staunchly by his mother's side and the media will carefully note and duly report that tears roll down Bobby's face as he bends to kiss his father's coffin.

Later, Bobby would tell Kennedy biographers Harrison Rainie and John Quinn, "It was not easy to have public attention so riveted on you in the worst moments of your life."

In 1738, Jonathan Swift wrote, "I always love to begin a journey on Sundays, because I shall have the prayers of the church, to preserve all that travel by land, or by water."

RFK's namesake son, Robert Francis Jr., began his unpredictable and ofttimes precarious journey through life on a Sunday, specifically January 17, 1954. Bobby was RFK and Ethel's third child and second son, and was given his father's name. Bobby's older brother Joseph had been named for their war hero uncle and august grandfather, both of whom were named Joe Kennedy.

The old adage that tells us "the rich are different" can definitely be applied to Bobby Kennedy and his childhood. Like many other kids, Bobby was an animal lover and had a dog—a black Newfoundland named Brumus—when he was a child. But Bobby was a *Kennedy*, and thus his love of animals was indulged to a degree beyond that of most adolescents. Bobby not only had a dog; he also took care of a "homeless" sixty-pound sea lion which he kept in the pool at the Kennedy family home at Hickory Hill in McLean, Virginia. His always amenable father had experts from the Bronx Zoo build Bobby a fully-functional terrarium in the basement of their family home. At one point, Bobby had seventy-five different breeds of animals in his do-it-yourself zoo, including monitor lizards, Chinese water dragons, and an array of snakes. In 1995, Bobby's cousin Chris Lawford told *New York* magazine, "Bobby was lord of that jungle and he could spend hours with it."

Bobby, who liked animals more than people when he was growing up, wrote a seventy-five-page book about animals when he was twelve years old, and once worked part-time during the summer at the National Zoo. Bobby also kept falcons and hawks at Hickory Hill. He fed the falcons bathtubs of raw meat. Once after being chastised by one of his cousins about how cruel it was to allow the mice and locusts he had brought as food for his predators to be eaten alive, he infested the house when he "freed" one thousand of these small creatures.

As a young man, Bobby was a notorious practical joker, and there were times when his jokes and pranks would turn cruel and hurtful. In an act completely out of character for an animal lover, he once gave his parakeet LSD. At his brother David's thirteenth birthday party, Bobby maliciously spiked everyone's milk with a laxative.

The young Bobby was also smart and charmingly self-deprecating at times, once telling a reporter he wanted to grow up to be a sanitation engineer. "It was important for my father to teach us how to take a joke and how to be laughed at," he said in *Growing Up Kennedy*. "A lot of people think that is just part of the 'spoiled Kennedys'—pushing people in swimming pools and the like. But it was important not to take yourself too seriously."

Sometimes, though, Bobby's jokes caused people a great deal of anxiety and pain. During his teens, Bobby once called his governess' boyfriend and, with grave seriousness, told him that his girlfriend had died. At a memorial Mass for his father, Bobby signaled his friend Phil Kirby, who was serving as an altar boy, to ring a bell at the wrong time, deliberately humiliating him in front of the assembled Kennedys and friends. Another time, at a prewedding party for his sister Mary Courtney, Bobby told his cousin Chris Lawford to make a hostage joke during the toast. (This was during the Iran hostage crisis.) The joke, of course, bombed, and Bobby led the jeers against a crestfallen Chris. Again, this was a deliberate and calculated public humiliation of a cousin.

Bobby got away with all this because he was perceived as the leader of the male Kennedy cousins. He was a notorious risk-taker and jumped off a garage roof at the Kennedy compound when he was eleven, resulting in severe leg lacerations and a severed tendon. His injury required one hundred stitches, and LBJ sent flowers. "We were a large family, and doing dangerous things was a way of getting attention," Bobby told Kennedy biographers Rainie and Quinn. "If you wanted to get out of the shadow of an older brother, you jumped off the roof." Bobby, who was a charter member of the notorious gang, the "Hyannis Port Terrors," knew he lived dangerously as a young man, also telling Rainie and Quinn, "I take a lot of risks with my life, saying things and doing things that I know I shouldn't do or will come to regret."

Regarding the HPT's antics, Larry Newman, a Hyannis Port neighbor of the Kennedys, who was also quoted in *Growing Up Kennedy*, said, "[The Kennedy children] were inside devils and outside angels. In essence they could do pretty much anything they wanted when they were home and in the neighborhood. . . . I think they believed there were two sets of rules governing the world: the one for the rest of us and the one for them."

Bobby's teenage years were turbulent. He almost ran away from home when he was sixteen, and in 1971, he was arrested in Hyannis for spitting at a cop. After transferring from Georgetown Prep to the Millbrook School, Bobby was expelled when he was fifteen for bad behavior.

He temporarily lived with the Brode family in Massachu-

setts during his senior year at the Palfrey School in Water-
town, yet another in a string of elite boarding schools his
mother sent him to as an attempt at straightening him out.
By this time Bobby, like his brother David (who Bobby described in 1995 as "my best friend"), was using drugs on a
regular basis, but stopped briefly when he lived with the
Brodes.

Because he was a Kennedy, Bobby was given many opportunities for very high-profile projects and endeavors when
he was in his early twenties, most notably hosting a TV special
and having his Harvard senior thesis published as a book. As
Bobby has acknowledged, his name provides opportunities for
him and he has admitted to doing "some traveling on it."
    In the fall of 1971, Bobby entered Harvard as a freshman,
ultimately graduating and moving on to the University of Virginia law school, where he earned his law degree.
    At Harvard, Bobby chose to write his honors thesis on
an important Alabama Federal judge named Frank Johnson.
He diligently studied the judge's life and work, including traveling to Alabama to research his achievements. This trip
starkly delineated for Bobby the significance of his heritage
and the mantle he wore because of his last name, when he
visited the Alabama legislature as part of his research, everyone wanted to meet him—simply because of whose son and
nephew he was.
    Shortly after his thesis was finished, fate and synchronicity
happily conspired to help Bobby become a published author.
When then-president Jimmy Carter named Judge Johnson
the head of the FBI, Putnam immediately offered Bobby a
deal to expand his thesis into a full-blown biography of the
judge. Bobby agreed and in 1978, *Judge Frank M. Johnson, Jr.:
A Biography* was published.
    The illustrious historian Arthur Schlesinger Jr. wrote the
jacket copy for Bobby's book: "[Kennedy] has given us a

vivid portrait, drawn with literary grace and historical detail, of a southern individualist who changed the life of Alabama." The respected trade publication *Library Journal* "highly recommended" the book in its review.

Bobby appeared on *The Mike Douglas Show* to promote the book, but not everyone was delighted with his debut effort. *The Boston Globe* and *The New York Times* in particular gave the book what Bobby described as "lousy reviews."

Unfortunately, any synergistic benefit Bobby could have gotten from Johnson's elevation to the head of the FBI was lost when the judge suffered an aneurism and a hernia and withdrew his acceptance.

On Sunday, September 7, 1975, Bobby appeared as the on-camera host for the television special, *The Last Frontier,* a show about wildlife produced by TV veteran Roger Ailes which ran on ABC and for which Bobby was paid several hundred thousand dollars. At the age of twenty-one, Bobby was remarkably poised and confident and did not seem at all spooked by the notion of hosting a TV documentary. Bobby's grandmother, Rose, was particularly proud of his high-profile achievement.

In the early eighties, when Bobby was in his twenties, he was scoring heroin in Harlem and using drugs on a regular basis. In September 1983, at the age of twenty-eight, he was arrested for heroin possession after he was found drugged and incoherent in an airplane bathroom on a flight to Deadwood, South Dakota. He immediately entered a rehab program at the Fair Oaks Hospital in Summit, New Jersey (the same drug treatment facility that treated singer John Phillips and his daughter actress Mackenzie Phillips), and issued a statement to the media in which he admitted using drugs and stated that he was going to face this problem head-on. He pled guilty to possession and was sentenced to two years probation and community service. This episode was the turning point for Bobby Jr., and he made a deliberate and concerted effort to straighten out his life. He ultimately succeeded, and in June 1985, he passed the New York bar exam, starting him on a life path that would include children, a happy marriage, and a passionate and vigorous defense of the environment.

Today, Bobby Kennedy Jr. does not do drugs or drink, and does not like to talk about his second and third decades. According to Pat Weschler, a journalist who interviewed Bobby in 1995 for a major profile in *New York* magazine titled "Nature Boy," "[Bobby] becomes visibly shaken when the subject is raised."

"Let's just say, I had a tumultuous adolescence that lasted until I was 29," he told Weschler, "and then I grew up very quickly." He also told *New York*, "There are certain things I wish I didn't have to live through, but . . . I have loved being a Kennedy."

In April 1982, Bobby married Emily Black, a pretty Protestant from Indiana whom Bobby convinced to convert to Roman Catholicism. They had two children, Robert Francis III, now eleven, and Kathleen Alexandra, seven. The family calls little Kathleen "Kick"—in memory of Bobby's aunt Kathleen, who died in 1948 in an airplane crash.

Bobby and Emily separated in 1992, and in March 1994, Bobby flew to the Dominican Republic for a quick divorce. A couple of weeks after the divorce, Bobby married his current wife, Mary Richardson, who now works as an architect for the New York design firm Parish Hadley.

Bobby and Mary have two children, Conor, two, and Kyra, one, and live in a farmhouse in Mount Kisco, New York. Bobby is on good terms with his first wife, Emily, with whom he shares custody of Bobby III and Kick.

Of his second wife, Mary, Bobby told *New York*, "If I could interview every woman on the planet, I couldn't find a woman more in sync with me."

Today, Bobby is a lawyer and activist whose main focus

is evironmental law—especially protecting water supplies. He also teaches environmental law at Pace University in White Plains, New York, and has admitted to flirting with the idea of joining the "family business" by getting into politics. "If I thought I could accomplish more in the political process," he told *New York* magazine, "I would." He also said, "I love politics. I always have a relative running, and I work in every campaign. I haven't ruled it out. But right now, I have a new wife and young children. I don't feel like I have to think about it for a couple of years."

Bobby has publicly said that he was speaking for his family when he stated that he did not think the JFK assassination case should be reopened.

Bobby is very close to his cousin, actor Chris Lawford, and the two men and their families see each other a lot. Chris has been quoted as saying, "I love Bobby, but I wouldn't want to be his wife. With Bobby, you always have to keep moving, keep those demons away."

Now, in his mid-forties, Bobby Kennedy Jr. has clearly found effective ways to keep the gates closed and the demons outside in the dark. One can't help but wonder, however, if he doesn't hear those demons baying at him every now and then on those nights when thoughts of his father and brothers—perhaps even his uncle—dance around in his mind.

David Anthony Kennedy

(June 15, 1955–April 25, 1984)

THE DEATH OF YELLOW DOVE

Whom the gods wish to destroy they first call promising.
—CYRIL CONNOLLY, *Enemies of Promise.*

On Wednesday, April 25, 1984, just before noon, David Anthony Kennedy—RFK's fourth child and third son—was found dead of a drug overdose in a $292-a-night suite in the Brazilian Court Hotel in Palm Beach, Florida, by the hotel bell captain and the hotel's desk clerk. He was two months away from his twenty-ninth birthday.

When David Anthony Kennedy was seven years old, his uncle Jack, the president of the United States, gave him a photograph as a gift. It was a picture of David standing in front of the White House, and on the picture, JFK had written, "A future President inspects his property."

How could such a promising Kennedy male, a young man JFK himself thought could aspire to the White House, have gone so wrong?

What happened to David Anthony Kennedy?

❋   ❋   ❋

124

Bobby and Ethel Kennedy's fourth child, David, was born on Wednesday, June 15, 1955, just a few months before the birth of his cousin Maria Shriver. Even though the two Kennedy cousins shared the same birth year, their lives took markedly different paths, with David's tragically ending prematurely.

When David was about eight years old, his father would tease him about his lisp and about liking wildflowers. David was a sensitive child, and he and his father shared a special bond because, as Kennedy biographers Peter Collier and David Horowitz noted in *The Kennedys: An American Drama,* "both were the runts of the litter."

RFK's third boy lived a short and sordid life. Hindsight tells us that David was probably overwhelmed by the violent death of his father, by the onus of being a Kennedy, and just by life itself. At the age of twelve, David had witnessed his father's shooting while watching coverage of the 1968 Democratic convention on TV, and was quoted as saying, "Oh, man, it's over . . . they got him, too."

David's behavior during his adolescence was often reprehensible. He was extremely rowdy as a teen and was a member of the notorious "Hyannis Port Terrors" a group of amphetamine-popping Kennedy brothers and cousins and their friends who threw rocks at cars, put M-80s and cherry bombs in neighbors' mailboxes, and beached expensive boats, apparently just for the fun of it. The HPTs also included David, Bobby Kennedy Jr., and Chris Lawford.

David was a risk-taker as a child and a teenager, often deliberately putting himself in harm's way (like risking electrocution or decapitation by jumping *much* too high on a trampoline that was positioned beneath a cable car), seemingly oblivious to the dangers. On May 30, 1968, shortly after his father's assassination, David was pulled under the waves at the beach in front of director John Frankenheimer's house during a visit there with his family. His brother Bobby had to dive in and rescue him.

David also seemed fascinated by the gruesome and the macabre. Following his father's funeral Mass, RFK's body was transported by train to its burial site in Arlington National Cemetery in Washington, DC. There was an enormous amount of media attention surrounding the funeral, and huge crowds lined the streets and thronged the train station. A terrible tragedy occurred when two people, eager to catch a glimpse of RFK's funeral train, were struck and violently killed by an oncoming train, in full view of David and the rest of his family. David was mesmerized by the bloody, lurid scene and the dead bodies, and had to be pulled away from the train window where he stood staring.

His father's death seemed to be the beginning of David's decline and ultimate demise. At his thirteenth birthday party, only two weeks after the assassination, David delighted in the fact that his prankster brother Bobby spiked everyone's milk with a laxative. Shortly thereafter, his mother Ethel sent thirteen-year-old David to a tennis and ski camp in Austria where he claimed to have had sex with a seventeen-year-old girl who was overwhelmed by the fact that he was a Kennedy. Upon his return to the States, David's brother Bobby turned him on to mescaline for the first time.

Ethel's response to David's troubled psyche was to withdraw: she refused to talk to him about his father's death, which David claimed to have foreseen in a dream. She did take him to see a psychiatrist, however, apparently hoping to transfer the burden of David's problems onto a professional. Given David's worsening drug problems and disaffection, the therapy does not seem to have worked.

During the Christmas season of 1969, *Time* magazine published a collection of remembrances about RFK by his children. David wrote the following about his father:

Daddy was very funny in church because he would embarrass all of us by singing very loud. Daddy did not have a very good voice. There will be no more football with Daddy, no more swimming with him, no more riding and no more camping with him. But he was the best father their [sic] ever was and I would rather have him for a father for the length of time I did than any other father for a million years.

It was at this time that David hitchhiked to New York City with his cousin Chris Lawford, scored heroin in Central Park, and moved into Chris' mother Pat's unused and vacant Fifth Avenue apartment. It wasn't long before the two cousins opened the apartment to a sundry assortment of destitute street people and conniving drug dealers. It took the outraged complaints of Pat's well-to-do neighbors to get them all out. By this time David was a regular user of cocaine and heroin, and when he moved back to Hickory Hill, he began to grow marijuana on the grounds there, as well.

In the summer of 1971, Ethel Kennedy arranged for David to stay at the Blackfoot Indian Reservation in Montana. She thought the experience might help ground him and teach him some self-discipline. The tribe members christened David "Yellow Dove" and attempted to teach him the ways of their people, but their influence seems to have been marginal at best. Ever hopeful, Ethel also arranged for David to pick lettuce with Cesar Chavez's workers during the summer of 1972, but that sojourn did little to transform David either.

In 1972, David was prescribed morphine for the severe pain he experienced following a Jeep accident in which his friend Pam Kelley was left paralyzed from the waist down. David fractured his vertebra in the accident and was placed in traction in the hospital. According to Ethel Kennedy biographer Jerry Oppenheimer, David took "as much [morphine] as he could get." At this point David claimed he was a "chipper"—someone who used heroin for fun but could stop at anytime.

After he recovered from the accident, David went to work part-time at the Nashville *Tennessean* newspaper. One widely told story about David's first days there emphasized how addicted he actually was at this point. Witnesses told of seeing syringes and packets of heroin fall out of the then-eighteen-year-old's jacket when he removed it.

David, who was now fascinated with rebel gonzo journalist Hunter Thompson, shot heroin all during his senior year of high school, and went on a forty-day drug shooting binge in 1976 that put him in the hospital with pneumonia and inflamed lymph glands.

David, who told friends at this point in his life that he was modeling himself after James Caan's character in the movie *The Gambler*, ultimately reenrolled at Harvard and began seeing a psychiatrist. The shrink prescribed Percodan for David, thinking David could use the powerful painkiller to wean himself off heroin. By late 1976 he had dropped out of Harvard and was living back at Hickory Hill.

In April 1978, he overdosed on Dilaudid and cocaine, and his mother sent him to England where he was given Neuro Electric Therapy, a fringe electrical current treatment that the Who's Peter Townshend swore by.

In the summer of 1978, in yet another bizarre incident in David's short life, he claimed he had a bloody fight with an intruder at Hickory Hill. The truth was that he had freaked out on drugs and made it look like someone had broken in and tried to rob him.

In early 1979, when David was twenty-four, he took money from his trust fund and moved to New York City, where he rented a penthouse on East Seventy-second Street and devoted himself to an orgiastic binge of drugs and sex. He began dating the actress Rachel Ward and once got into a fistfight with Princess Caroline's husband Phillipe Junot at the club Xenon because he imagined Junot was pursuing Rachel. During this period, David was supplementing his heroin usage with forty Percodans a day—usage that would almost immediately kill a nonaddict. Every week, David would travel to Cambridge, Massachusetts, where his psychiatrist, Dr. Lee Macht, would give him five prescriptions for forty Percodans each. Back in New York, he would go from pharmacy to pharmacy, filling each prescription, thereby assuring himself of at least a five-day supply of narcotics.

Life in New York went on like this for the better part of that year until September 1979, when he was beaten bloody while trying to score heroin in Harlem. Drug dealers called David "White James" because of his James Caan fixation. His family intervened and had him sent to the McLean Hospital in Boston, where he went through a drug rehabilitation program. He ended up being sent to Massachusetts General, though, when it was discovered that he was also suffering from a very dangerous condition called bacterial endocarditis, which he had contracted from using dirty needles.

Following his release from Massachusetts General, David agreed to enter a year-long drug program in Sacramento, California, called the Aquarian Effort. His family insisted that David pay the program's $100,000 annual fee with his own money, and David was livid that the family wouldn't pick up the tab. During his stay in California, his mother occasionally visited him. At one point, David actually considered attending his father's assassin Sirhan Sirhan's parole hearing.

After he "graduated" from the Aquarian Effort, David remained in California and temporarily worked in a construction job he got thanks to Frank Gifford's daughter, and even sold Amway, but at this time he was living mainly on $2,000 a month drawn from his Kennedy trust fund. Even though he was technically "clean and sober," David's addictive tendencies would not allow him to stay straight. He began deliberately putting himself into hypoglycemic states by drinking without eating, causing him to get shaky and hallucinate.

In the fall of 1982, David left Sacramento and moved to the Beacon Hill section of Boston, taking an apartment with Paula Sculley, a fashion photographer he was dating. He began working as an intern at *Atlantic Monthly* magazine and reenrolled at Harvard, but dropped out after one semester. This period of attempted renewal and recovery was short-lived, and David ultimately went back to drugs. He once again needed hospitalization, and in March of 1984 was admitted to St. Mary's Rehabilitation Center in Minneapolis, register-ing under the name of David Kilroy. Upon his release in April, he traveled to Palm Beach, where he took a room at the Brazilian Court Hotel. He visited his grandmother Rose, then spent his days drinking and doing drugs until the morn-ing of April 25, when David Kennedy's short life came to its sad and pathetic conclusion.

One of the drugs found in David's system during his au-topsy was liquid Demerol, a very potent and highly addictive painkiller. It was later learned that David had stolen a large vial of this drug two days earlier from his ailing grandmother Rose Kennedy's bedside. The other drugs in his system at the time of his death were high-grade, almost uncut, cocaine, and the powerful tranquilizer Mellaril.

Regarding the theft of the Demerol from Rose's room, Rose Kennedy's former secretary Barbara Gibson, in her 1993 Thunder's Mouth Press book *The Kennedys: The Third Genera-tion*, wrote:

According to individuals who were present, it is be-lieved that David did not take the Demerol from his grandmother. . . . According to the staff, the Demerol seemed to be missing after a visit by Caroline Ken-nedy and Sydney Lawford. No one has said for cer-tain that the Demerol was present just prior to their appearance in the room, and that it was missing just after they left. However, the staff opinion is that one of the two girls was involved in taking it, not David.

Gibson also wrote that, "if they were the ones who gave him the Demerol, they did it because, in their own minds, [they believed] it would help."

The autopsy also found needle marks in David's groin and noted that his right sock was on inside out. These facts led to an investigation to determine whether or not someone had been in David's room after his death. Suspicions arose that someone had "cleaned up" the hotel suite, dressed David, and disposed of drugs. Analysis of the water in the room's toilet bowl turned up traces of cocaine and Demerol. Also, 1.3 grams of cocaine were ultimately found in the room during the investigation.

The suggested macabre scenario had one or more people visiting David in his hotel room and finding him naked or partially dressed, lying on the floor with a syringe sticking out of his groin, dead from an overdose. These "mystery visitors" were suspected of being people whom David knew— individuals involved with the Kennedy family who had an interest in protecting the clan from the certain scandal which would result from the details of such a grisly and sordid crime scene being released to the public.

David's two cousins, Caroline Kennedy, then twenty-six, and Sydney Lawford McKelvy, twenty-seven, two young women with whom he was very close, were the family members who identified his body and were questioned by the police after David's body was found. Both denied being anywhere near the hotel on the day of David's death, even though the bell captain told police that the two had been seen near David's room about an hour and a half before the hotel received a phone call from David's mother Ethel Kennedy asking someone from the hotel to check on her son.

David had been scheduled to catch a plane to Boston that morning. He had called his girlfriend Paula in Boston at 9:00 A.M. on the morning of his death and told her he had decided to attend Alcoholics Anonymous meetings and that he was returning to Boston. He told her to expect him. He had been on a drinking binge since he had arrived in Palm Beach. Ethel Kennedy told the hotel clerk that she wanted to be sure David had checked out on time and gotten on the plane, and asked him to please enter David's room to make sure he had left.

Conspiracy theorists speculate that Caroline and Sydney were the ones who visited David, found him naked and dead, and then dressed him, flushed drugs down the toilet, and removed drug paraphernalia from the room. It was also suspected that they then called his mother. An unnamed witness also alleged to police that Caroline and Sydney had both *admitted* to removing two syringes and a packet of cocaine from David's room before Ethel's call. During police questioning, both cousins steadfastly denied entering David's room or having any involvement with a coverup involving his death. The matter was closed. In a sworn statement released January 14, 1985 by Palm Beach County State Attorney David Bludworth, Caroline denied personally entering David's room at any time.

A few months later after David's funeral, two men who worked as bellhops at the Brazilian Court Hotel were charged with selling cocaine to David.

After the autopsy, David's body was returned to his family, and on Friday, April 27, 1984, he was buried next to his grandfather, Joe Kennedy, at Holyhood Cemetery in Brookline, Massachusetts.

At David's funeral, the guests were given a blue Mass card featuring a drawing that David had done for his father's funeral when he was thirteen years old. David had used the John Donne line, "Death be not proud," and the quotation resonated among the family members and friends who had also attended RFK's funeral.

Noelle Fell, one of Ethel Kennedy's secretaries during the seventies, is quoted in *The Other Mrs. Kennedy* as stating that David was Ethel's least favorite child. David seemed to know this intuitively, and he also believed that the rest of his family considered him a black sheep. During his stay in Sacramento, David sat for an interview with Kennedy biographers Peter Collier and David Horowitz for their book *The Kennedys: An American Drama*. He told them about sitting on the bank of the Sacramento River one day, drinking wine with his friends and flipping through an issue of *High Times* magazine. He came across a picture of his Aunt Rosemary that was part of an article about lobotomies. "The thought crossed my mind," he said, "that if my grandfather was alive, the same thing could have happened to me that happened to her. She was an embarrassment; I am an embarrassment. She was a hindrance; I am a hindrance. As I looked at this picture, I began to hate my grandfather and all of them for having done the thing they had done to her and for doing the thing they were doing to me."

Collier and Horowitz also recount another telling David Kennedy moment. Later, during a newspaper interview, when asked by a reporter what his mother would like him to be, David had bitterly replied, "President."

Mary Courtney Kennedy

(b. September 9, 1956)

A BORN FIGHTER

The Kennedys are born fighters and we are all proud of it.
—MARY COURTNEY, writing in *That Shining Hour*, Pat Lawford's privately-published tribute to her brother, RFK

Mary Courtney Kennedy Hill, called "Courtney," to distinguish her from her sister Mary Kerry (called "Kerry"), is the only female member of the younger generation of Kennedys who is married to a man who was once convicted of murder. At least that's how the media has often described Courtney following her second marriage, to convicted Irish Republican Army terrorist Paul Hill, in 1993. Courtney had divorced first husband Jeff Ruhe in 1990.

Paul Hill was a member of the so-called "Guildford Four," a group believed responsible for a deadly pub bombing in October 1974 in Great Britain. Hill and his three fellow Guildford Four members were convicted following a trial, but the convictions were overturned in 1989 after Hill and his three cohorts had been imprisoned for fifteen years. Hill ultimately confessed to the bombing after an unrelenting period of harsh interrogation, an ordeal that resulted in Hill also confessing to the murder of Brian Shaw, a former British soldier who had been kidnapped from a British pub in July 1974. The truth was that Hill wasn't responsible for either the bombing or the murder he was accused of.

March 21, 1994, *People* magazine published a lengthy feature titled "Being Green," about a trip members of the Kennedy family made to Ireland to attend Paul's appeal on his conviction of Brian Shaw's murder. Ethel, Courtney, Joe II, Rory, Kathleen, and Kerry were among the RFK family members who visited Belfast for the trial. "I know I'm innocent," Hill told reporters. "I want to clear my name." Representative Joe Kennedy also spoke out about why the Kennedys were present in such numbers: "We just hope that Paul—an Irish Catholic—can get justice in Northern Ireland. Our Irishness is fundamental and instinctive," he went on. "It is not something we were taught." Family matriarch Ethel Kennedy also spoke to the assembled media: "We're like any other Irish-Catholic family. We rally when in trouble." Ethel was also quoted in Jerry Oppenheimer's biography *The Other Mrs. Kennedy* as saying, "Paul's one of us now, a Kennedy. No one pushes Kennedys around."

Shortly after the Kennedy family's visit to Ireland, Paul Hill's conviction for the murder of Brian Shaw was overturned by Belfast's High Court. Paul Hill ultimately went on to write a successful book about his unjust imprisonment titled, appropriately, *Stolen Years*. The story of the Guildford Four's wrongful imprisonment—and their questionable interrogation by authorities—was dramatized in the 1993 film *In the Name of the Father*, starring Daniel Day-Lewis and Emma Thompson.

Courtney Kennedy met Paul Hill after her mother Ethel Kennedy asked Hill to visit Courtney when she was laid up in the hospital following a skiing accident. Hill had previously been introduced to Ethel Kennedy by her son Joe. As soon as Ethel met Hill, she immediately felt that he would be perfect for Courtney.

Courtney and Paul Hill hit it off almost immediately and the two were married in the Aegean Sea on the yacht the *Varmar VE* in July 1993. "I love Paul," Courtney told a family friend. "He's the most magnetic man I've ever met!" After they were wed, the couple lived in County Clare, Ireland, for about a year before returning to the United States, where they lived in Courtney's luxurious Fifth Avenue apartment in Manhattan.

Mary Courtney Kennedy was Ethel and RFK's second daughter after the birth of their eldest child Kathleen, and the first girl born after the male trio of Joe II, Bobby Jr., and David. She was named after her mother Ethel's college friend, Courtney Murphy Benoist. Like many of her cousins, Courtney attended Our Lady of Victory School in Washington, DC, the Stone Ridge School, then the prestigious Potomac School. She studied history and literature at the University of California and also took a few courses at Trinity College in Dublin.

Courtney was barely twelve when her father was assassinated, and like many of her siblings and cousins, she expressed her pain with an essay for *That Shining Hour,* writing that "Daddy loved us all. He did everything he could to be with us . . ."

Courtney, now a human rights activist, has been interested in social issues since she was quite young. As an adolescent she volunteered to work in programs to help inner-city youth, and she also was involved in the Head Start and Very Special Arts programs when she was in her teens and twenties. (She was working as a goodwill ambassador for a Rome-based AIDS foundation at the time of her marriage to Hill.)

In 1980, at the age of twenty-four, Courtney was working

as a production assistant for ABC-TV's Children's Television Workshop. During her time with the Workshop, she met Jeff Ruhe, a vibrant young man who was then working as an assistant to Roone Arledge, the president of ABC-TV news and sports division. Shortly afterwards, the two married on June 26, 1980. As the eldest male of the family, Uncle Ted once again had the honor of giving away the bride. Courtney and Jeff Ruhe's marriage lasted ten years, and in 1990, Courtney achieved the dubious distinction of being the first Kennedy grandchild to divorce.

Courtney Kennedy Hill seems to deliberately keep a low profile. Even though she has been involved in some volatile situations due to her husband's involvement with the IRA, she rarely appears in a public forum and remarks by her are almost impossible to find. She is one of the less-visible Kennedy grandchildren, and even though her stalwart defense and support of her husband would suggest the possibility of some kind of political involvement, Courtney instead seems to prefer channeling her energies into global human rights issues through activist organizations rather than through elected office. She does not participate in articles profiling the younger generation of Kennedys. Other than the media coverage of her and her family's trip to Ireland in support of Hill, there has been almost no mention of her in the press for quite some time.

Courtney and Paul Hill have been married since 1993 and have one daughter named Saoirse Roisin, Irish Gaelic for "Freedom Rose."

Michael LeMoyne Kennedy

(February 27, 1958–December 31, 1997)

QUESTIONS OF JUDGMENT

Every one of his brothers and sisters, his mother and all our family, turned to him again and again. And he turned, heart and soul, to the task our father set, which has inspired each of us and people everywhere—to make more gentle the life of [the] world.

—from JOSEPH KENNEDY II's eulogy for his brother Michael

Michael LeMoyne Kennedy's death in a skiing accident on New Year's Eve, 1997, brought to a tragic close a year in which his promising future was threatened by a sex scandal that put his name on the front page of every newspaper in America.

While skiing on the slopes of the Aspen Mountain resort in Colorado, Michael slammed headfirst into a birch tree, resulting in massive head and neck injuries that were later described in an autopsy report released by coroner Rob Kurtzman as "instantaneous and incapacitating." Kurtzman also reported that death occurred in "seconds to minutes." The autopsy report also revealed that no traces of alcohol, amphetamines, barbiturates, marijuana, cocaine, or opium were found in Michael Kennedy's system at the time of his death.

Michael and other family members had been playing ski football, passing back and forth a blue plastic football while skiing down icy slopes that had been graded as groomed packed powder—very fast skiing conditions. Adding to the potential for an accident was the dwindling sunlight and the fact that Michael was skiing without ski poles, and was not wearing a helmet.

After Michael hit the tree, the ski patrol was called by walkie-talkie and were on the scene within four minutes. During that time, Michael's sister Rory performed CPR on her brother and Michael's children tearfully prayed the Lord's Prayer over him. As Michael was being ferried down the hill on a gondola, he lost his pulse and intensive first aid was performed. At the nearby Aspen Valley Hospital, doctors worked for an hour to save Michael, but to no avail. Last Rites were administered by Catholic priest Reverend Lawrence Sloan and Michael was pronounced dead at 5:50 P.M. His body was returned to Hyannis Port, Massachusetts on a chartered plane the following day and his wake was held at the Kennedy Compound on Friday, January 2. Michael's funeral was held at Our Lady of Victory Church in Cape Cod and his body was then driven to Brookline, Massachusetts where he was buried in the Kennedy family plot in Holyhood Cemetery, near his brother David and his grandparents.

Michael LeMoyne Kennedy was born on February 27, 1958. He weighed eight pounds and was sandwiched in birth order between his two sisters Mary Courtney and Mary Kerry. And since Michael was yet another male Kennedy scion, his arrival was celebrated by an elaborate photo layout in the April 24, 1958 issue of *Life* magazine.

As a child, Michael was rather precocious. When he was ten, he greeted a new employee at Hickory Hill with "Hiya.

You're our eleventh governess. How long you think you'll last?" Around the same time, he enjoyed answering his family's home phone with the words, "Confusion here." He was as Kennedy biographers Rainie and Quinn described him, the "vital center" of the RFK. children.

In *That Shining Hour,* the privately-published Kennedy family tribute to RFK after his death, Michael wrote this charmingly innocent remembrance of his father. He was only ten at the time:

> In the last part of his life, Daddy did everything he could for this country. He helped the Indians; he helped the Negro. He loved his country very much. He took us to see the wilderness of this country. He loved sports. We played football all the time when he was home. He did almost as much for his family as for his country. He had many different friends; some black, some white. He had a lot of professional athletes for friends. His country, his family and his friends all miss him very much.

As an adolescent, Michael attended the prestigious St. Paul's School, from which he graduated in 1975. In 1979, he graduated from Harvard, where he had studied his uncle JFK.'s administration. "The more I studied," he said of the experience, "the more I believed in what he did" (*Growing Up Kennedy*). He later graduated from the University of Virginia Law School and worked at the Washington, DC law firm Hogan and Hartson for a period before being made chairman of brother Joe's Citizen's Energy Corporation. He also ran his Uncle Ted's 1994 Senate reelection campaign and at that time many political mavens speculated that Michael himself would someday run for Congress. In December 1992, a Kennedy insider told *Cosmopolitan* magazine, "Michael's got it all. When he decides to get involved politically, he'll go right to the top." Michael always believed (as did many of the other younger Kennedys) that his family name brought responsibilities. "We saw the trappings of responsibility all around us," he once said. "We knew that our position brought responsibility".

In 1974, Michael was working as an intern in his uncle Ted's office where he met his future wife, Victoria Gifford, daughter of the sportscaster Frank Gifford. He had briefly dated Tatum O'Neal previously. After a seven-year courtship, they wed in 1981 in St. Ignatius Loyola Church in New York City. As Kennedy weddings are wont to, Michael and Vicki's nuptials got a lot of media attention, being a high-profile union of politics and Hollywood. The bridesmaids wore purple gowns made in Switzerland. Andy Warhol commented on the union: "She was the prettiest bride I've ever seen in my life. . . . It made you want to get married, it really did."

Michael and Vicki had three children, Michael Jr., Kyle, and Rory. At the time of Michael's death in 1997 they were fourteen, twelve, and nine years old, respectively. Michael's eldest son, Michael Jr., was one of his father's pallbearers.

Michael led a relatively quiet life until April 1997, when the thirty-nine-year-old's name exploded into the consciousness of American culture.

Unfortunately, this unexpected media blitz focusing on Michael was coverage of yet another Kennedy scandal, this one involving alleged statutory rape, alcoholism, and divorce. Michael, who earlier in his life had had trouble with drug use and self-destructive behavior often centering around risky, daredevil-type activities, had, for the most part, been one of the quieter, less-known Kennedys.

Then, on Friday, April 25, 1997, in an article that would be quickly picked up by the national media, the *Boston Globe* reported that unnamed neighbors of Michael and his wife Victoria Gifford Kennedy alleged that Michael had had an illicit affair with a local girl—who had been the Kennedys' babysitter since she was twelve. Now nineteen and a student

at Boston University, the girl and her family initially had
nothing to say and did not confirm or deny the allegations of
the neighbors.

According to the *Boston Globe* story, the affair allegedly
started when the girl was just fourteen and continued on and
off for five years. In January 1995, Michael's wife Victoria
allegedly caught the two lovers in bed in the Kennedy home
in Cohasset, Massachusetts. The report said that Michael
claimed the rendezvous was a result of his ongoing alcoholism
and he agreed to enter an alcohol rehab program. "I've come
to recognize I had a dependence on alcohol," Michael said in a
released statement shortly thereafter that year. "I am currently
participating in a program and I am committed to completing
it this month." Kennedy family matriarch Rose Kennedy, Michael's grandmother, had died in January 1995. Michael had
not attended her funeral because he was trying to complete
his rehab program at Father Martin's Ashley Center in Maryland on the day of the funeral.

On April 17, 1997, Michael and Victoria released a statement that they were separating. "We have reached this decision amicably," the joint statement read. "Out of respect for
our families, we hope the press and public will understand
our wish to decline further comment on this matter."

The Saturday after the *Boston Globe* broke the story, they
ran a follow-up story headlined, "Norfolk authorities begin
investigation of Kennedy kin." The report confirmed that authorities could not proceed with an indictment against Michael
Kennedy for statutory rape until they spoke with the alleged
victim. The report acknowledged that it would be very difficult for a district attorney to pursue charges against Michael
if the girl refused to cooperate or was not forthcoming with
her version of the alleged relationship.

The authorities faced several obstacles in prosecuting Michael Kennedy. First was the fact that the alleged affair was
more than likely consensual. This would not eliminate the

statutory rape charge but it did throw up a roadblock to putting together an effective case. Another problem was the close relationship between the family of the babysitter and Michael and Victoria Kennedy's family. The possibility existed that the two families would resolve the matter privately, and stay mum to any and all inquiries. Perhaps for all these reasons, no charges were ultimately filed against Michael in connection with the incident.

Regardless of the outcome of this particular case, however, the Kennedy name was embroiled in scandal once again. Moreover, the media used this opportunity to run full-page features rehashing the many past scandals of the family. The New York *Daily News* had a page titled "The Kennedy Capers: Kennedy Sex Scandals" and ran photos of Joe Kennedy and Gloria Swanson; JFK and Judith Exner; Ted Kennedy and Mary Jo Kopechne; RFK and Marilyn Monroe; and, of course, William Kennedy Smith.

Kennedy watchers began speculating on whether or not Michael's troubles would affect his brother Joe's run for Massachusetts governor. "This isn't Joe, but it has the potential for keeping alive the issue of Kennedy men and family values," University of Massachusetts McCormack Institute fellow Lou DiNatale told *USA Today*. Joe subsequently did drop out of the race.

On Monday, January 5, 1998, two days after Michael's funeral, TV host Kathie Lee Gifford, wife of Michael's father-in-law, Frank Gifford, announced on her show *Live with Regis and Kathie Lee* that Michael had passed three lie detector tests earlier in the year. Even though Michael's reported affair with the babysitter was wrong, Kathie Lee admitted, it was *not* criminal because the polygraph tests had indicated that Michael had not had sex with the girl until she was of legal age.

Following his death, the Associated Press also reported that Michael and Vicki were attempting a reconciliation and that Michael had met in recent weeks with a Boston public relations specialist to discuss ways of rehabilitating his tainted image.

In *Growing Up Kennedy,* a friend of Michael's told the authors that Michael's philosophy was to immediately "forge ahead" after he decided to do something. If you hesitate, the friend says Michael believed, "hesitation then becomes the danger."

The babysitter scandal forced Michael to learn the hard way that sometimes hesitation can be less dangerous than forging ahead with a reckless decision. Michael's tragic death during a reckless and dangerous game sadly reemphasizes that he had not taken to heart lessons recently learned.

Mary Kerry Kennedy

(b. September 8, 1959)

TSAH WAKIE WALKING THE AISLE ALONE

I remember sitting in front of the TV and watching Washington burn after the assassination of Martin Luther King Jr. And my father was trying to explain how very, very close this was and why people were doing this—that while the actions were wrong, the reasons for it were understandable and that we had some sort of responsibility for that.
—KERRY KENNEDY, in the June 7, 1993 issue of *People*
magazine

Not much fun but great last names.
—*Time* magazine's capsule summary of workaholics Kerry Kennedy and Andrew Cuomo in a 1994 tongue-in-cheek ranking of Washington power couples

A lot of kids talk about what they want to be when they grow up. "I want to be a fireman," one little boy might say. "I want to be a doctor," a little girl might tell her parents. Kerry Kennedy was no different in this respect, except that she *was* different from most little kids simply by virtue of being a Kennedy: she was Rose and Joe's grandchild—and, perhaps more importantly, she was Robert F. Kennedy's daughter.

So when Kerry, at the age of seven, precociously told her father she wanted to be an Indian when she grew up, the Kennedy clout was wielded and Kerry was given the opportunity to experience something most kids that age could only read about. Kerry talked about this moment in the June 7, 1993 issue of *People* magazine:

> [My father's] concern for the poor also made him very special. When I was a child, his work with Native Americans was most inspiring to me. He would come home from a reservation and tell us about what he had seen. I'm told that when asked what I wanted to do when I grew up I would say, "I want to be an Indian." And in fact my father got a Comanche woman to come to our home and initiate me into the tribe when I was about 7. My name was Tsah Wakie (One who looks for the best in everything).

Mary Kerry Kennedy Cuomo as an adult has been described by no less a sociocultural observer than Arthur Schlesinger Jr. as "a powerhouse disguised as an ingenue."

Kerry (like her sister Mary Courtney, she uses her middle name to avoid confusion between them) is best known for being one-half of the marriage that united what many believe to be the two most powerful Democratic families in the United States. Kerry's June 9, 1990 wedding to Andrew Cuomo— son of former New York governor Mario Cuomo and current Secretary of Housing and Urban Development in the Clinton administration—received almost as much media attention as the unions of her cousins Caroline Kennedy and Maria Shriver with their own high-profile beaus. Columnist Mary McGrory wrote of this union, "The Kennedys have a history of overwhelming their in-laws, but there was a general feeling that, in the Cuomos, they had met their match. This obviously is a merger, not a takeover." The tabloids also weighed in on the marriage, dubbing it "Cuomolot."

Kerry, who herself described her marriage as a union of "passion and pragmatism," is nothing if not a free spirit and an independent thinker. She refused to have someone walk her down the aisle at her wedding, opting instead to march to the altar alone. One got the sense that neither Uncle Ted nor any of her beloved brothers would do—if her father couldn't do it, no one would. "She stuck to her guns," said Kennedy family friend, writer Art Buchwald. "She didn't want anyone to give her away."

Kerry and Andrew's decision to wed in St. Matthew's Cathedral could also be looked upon as a statement of sorts— an in-your-face refusal to let the past dominate and dictate to the present: St. Matthew's was where her slain uncle Jack's funeral had taken place twenty-seven years earlier. Revisiting that place had to have been extremely painful for Kerry's mother Ethel and likely even more so, of course, for Kerry's Aunt Jackie. But the hour-long ceremony took place there, with a total of forty-one bridesmaids, ushers, and flower girls in attendance. At her and Andrew's Hickory Hill wedding reception, three hundred guests dined on lamb and salmon, while dogs (yes, dogs) wearing satin bows wandered the estate grounds.

Ever since their "merger," Kerry Kennedy and Andrew Cuomo have been the textbook definition of a highly influential power couple, and with Cuomo's ascendancy to the powerful position of HUD secretary in 1997, the thirty-nine-year-old Italian-American began to be talked about as a vice presidential candidate, the running mate for Al Gore when he makes his expected run for the presidency in the year 2000. *If* Cuomo runs with Gore, and *if* Gore is elected in 2000 and reelected in 2004, and *if* Andrew Cuomo is the Democratic presidential candidate in 2008 and *if* he is elected, then Kerry Kennedy Cuomo would be the first "Kennedy" First Lady since Jackie. A lot of "ifs," for sure, but this scenario could play out in the highly volatile world of American politics.

There is no denying that Andrew Cuomo is a definite player whose name recognition at times rivals that of Kerry's—a development even Kerry has acknowledged, quoted in *The Kennedys: The Third Generation* as saying shortly after her marriage, "You know what's a relief? Ever since I got married, I've never met a reporter who didn't ask about my husband."

Kerry and Andrew have twin daughters, Mariah and Cara.

Growing up, Kerry—RFK and Ethel's seventh child—was especially close with her sister Kathleen and took comfort in her family's religious faith. "Religion is an important foundation for us all," Kerry said in *Growing Up Kennedy*. "It's an essential place to turn and in many ways has helped us all through some hard times."

Kerry graduated from the Putney School in 1977 and from Boston University in 1982. She earned her law degree from Boston College Law School in 1987 (she passed the Massachusetts bar exam on her first try) and in 1988, she founded the Robert F. Kennedy Memorial Center for Human Rights. She is currently the executive director of the center and also serves as the organization's legal counsel. After she graduated from college, Kerry's passion for helping the oppressed and the less fortunate manifested itself in volunteer work. She donated time to Amnesty International and focused her energies on human rights violations throughout the world, including personally helping Salvadoran refugees. Following her establishment of the RFK Center, Kerry personally led human rights missions to over a dozen countries, including Northern Ireland, Haiti, Kenya, Poland, and Chile. To commemorate the twenty-fifth anniversary of her father's death in 1993, Kerry scheduled a series of conferences jointly known as A

Vision for America. This program's purpose was to discuss the ways her father's dreams of opportunity and equality for all could be used in today's world.

"I . . . think the country would be different today had [my father] lived," Kerry told *People* magazine in 1993. "I think the Vietnam War would have ended a lot earlier and there would never have been a Watergate. His policies and programs really were devoted to the cities. He would be horrified by what he would see today—crack, violence, children having children—and I can only imagine some of these issues might have been addressed with a little bit more vigor."

Like many of her cousins, Kerry has also helped out, with her husband, of course, in her family's many political campaigns with the likes of Tom Hanks and President Bill Clinton. Whether or not Kerry Kennedy Cuomo ever ends up in the White House (one way or another) remains to be seen.

Regardless of her political future, it's likely that Kerry will continue to be an advocate for the advancement of human rights throughout the world and will always try to fulfill the legacy of her Native American name by looking for—and expecting—the best from others, whether those others happen to be people she comes into contact with working with the center dedicated to her father's work, or with governments who perpetuate injustice and human rights violations.

Christopher George Kennedy
(b. July 4, 1963)

A CHIP OFF GRANDPA JOE

Money gives you clear evidence of winning and losing. You either make money or you don't, and it's clear right then and there.
—CHRIS KENNEDY, espousing his grandfather Joe's philosophies

Even though Christopher George Kennedy is one of the two RFK children born on the fourth of July (sister Kathleen is the other), he is as far away from politics as a Kennedy can get: he is a businessman and seems to be perfectly content making money and growing the family's business instead of cultivating political cronies.

Chris has admitted that the lives of the RFK children who were very young when their father was killed (he was only five) have not been as dramatic or intense as the lives of those who were adolescents or teenagers at the time of the assassination. "We have not had the adventures or excitement or some of the problems the older ones have had," Chris once remarked. This statement might have been offered as Chris's attempt to explain why he does not seem to share the "calling" to politics and public service that his older siblings Kathleen, Joe II, and Bobby Jr. do.

Regardless of the reason, however, Chris is not interested in politics except tangentially, and there is no denying that he is very good at what *does* interest him: business.

Chris currently helps run the Kennedy family-owned Merchandise Mart in Chicago as vice president of marketing. The Merchandise Mart is a large and important furniture and trade center in the Midwest. He and his wife Sheila have three children—Katherine, Christopher, and Sarah—and avoid the limelight. He spends his days making money; one cannot help but feel that Grandpa Joe would be proud.

Chris was born on Independence Day in 1968 at 6:48 P.M., weighing six pounds, fourteen ounces. His proud father was quoted shortly after Chris' birth as saying, "They tell me he was the best-looking child ever born at St. Elizabeth's [Hospital in Boston]. He's got a strong face just like his grandfather. He's got a lot of character. He's a very good-looking baby. And, oh, he's got black hair."

Christopher was baptized a week later at St. Francis Xavier Church in Hyannis Port by Cardinal Richard Cushing. Chris, who was the only child of RFK who was born when JFK was in the White House, prompted his uncle the president to comment, "He looks like a pretty good baby, but of course, we'll know later."

As a youngster, Christopher George was quite the precocious lad. Kennedy family biographers Peter Collier and David Horowitz, in their book, *The Kennedys: An American Drama,* recount one amusing anecdote (credited to Bobby Jr. in their notes) from when Chris was five. Shortly after RFK was assassinated, John Kennedy Jr., apparently somewhat confused by yet another terrible tragedy and funeral taking place in the family, asked Christopher if his father would still be going to his office in the Senate every day. "Oh yes," Chris replied. "He's in heaven in the morning and he goes to his office in the afternoon."

Chris—a young man many familiar with the RFK kids feel was one of the most responsible of the brood even at an early age—started his own summer sailboat rental business at Hyannis Port when he was still in his teens. He also worked manning a hotline at a center for runaway children, often personally reaching out to youths in trouble, lending them money, and even inviting them back to Hickory Hill for a meal and a visit. He was considered one of the best counselors at the center. Chris may also have been somewhat compulsive in his early years. The story is told that a teenaged Chris once made a bunch of visiting adults pick up trash off the Hickory Hill grounds during an especially messy party.

Chris attended Georgetown Prep—he reportedly hated high school—earned his BA from Boston College, and an MBA from Northwestern University's Kellogg School. He briefly dated actress Tatum O'Neal, and married Sheila Berner in 1987. They have three children.

As a member of America's reigning political family, Chris has given thought to what it means to be a Kennedy. "You don't wake up and realize there's something strange about you," he once said. "But as a Kennedy you generate more interest than someone else. . . . We were taught that we've got advantages, and it is unfair that everybody does not have the same advantages. The important thing was to use our advantages in a way that makes it fairer for others."

Matthew Maxwell Taylor Kennedy

(b. January 11, 1965)

ELLIOT NESS

The environmental problem is not caused by people hunting but by businesses polluting, and they are the most powerful. In order to have any kind of effect on them, you have to know how they work.

— MAX KENNEDY, during his time at Harvard

One of the intriguing facets of the whole Kennedy picture is how usually contradictory elements often coexist in the daily lives of the many offspring of the Kennedy brothers and sisters. Matthew Maxwell Kennedy, known to family and friends as Max, is a representative of how this kind of paradigm works even accidentally: Max has worked in law enforcement, served as an assistant district attorney in Boston, and yet he was unwittingly involved, however tangentially, in the William Kennedy Smith/Palm Beach debacle, when one of his girlfriends claimed she was sexually assaulted by Max's cousin, Willie.

Of course, the girl's allegations had nothing to do with

Max, other than the fact that they were dating at the time. However, they illustrate not only the duality of the Kennedy family character but are also a good example of what makes *being* a Kennedy sometimes a trial.

Max's involvement with the William Kennedy Smith rape trial was, as noted, tangential. A girl Max was dating claimed that she too had been assaulted by Willie after a party in New York City. When the woman informed Willie that she was going to tell Max Kennedy what had happened, Willie allegedly replied, "Don't—that's not the way it happened." The following morning the woman called Max and told him what his cousin had done to her. But it was too late: Willie had already spoken with Max Kennedy, supposedly apologizing for his inappropriate advances. Reportedly, Max forgave Willie and perhaps tried to convince his girlfriend that she was blowing the incident out of proportion. The woman was later interviewed by the police when Willie was charged with rape.

When Max was born, the New York *Daily News* ran a front page headline telling the world that the birth of RFK and Ethel's ninth child "[Gave] Ethel and Bobby a Baseball Team!" Max was baptized a week later, on January 17, 1965. His big sister Kathleen and big brother Joe II, both then thirteen years old, served proudly as his godparents.

RFK had hopes that this sixth son of his would grow up to become a United States senator. Max was named after one of his father's heroes, General Maxwell G. Taylor, a notable military leader who later went on to serve as the United States Ambassador to South Vietnam.

Max was a tad rambunctious, and somewhat accident prone, as a child, and there are several fascinating "Max" stories recounted in various Kennedy biographies. In one incident, Max and his brother Chris had an embarrassing fistfight at one of RFK's press conferences when the two were just

toddlers (Max, four; Chris, six). Another time, Chris mischie-
vously suggested that Max spit crumbs all over an RFK female campaign worker's nice clean suit. Max gleefully obliged.
Max once injured his cousin Kara's friend Linda Semans
when he threw her a boat tow-rope handle—and accidentally
hit her in the head hard enough for her to require medical
attention. At seven, Max broke his leg in a bizarre accident
at Hyannis Port when a flagpole snapped in a strong wind
and landed on him. Some of his cousins and siblings had been
out sailing and upon their return, they ran their wet sail up
the pole to dry in the wind. The sail was so heavy, however,
that the wind snapped the pole and landed on little Max.

Shortly after his leg was broken by the falling flagpole,
Max fainted during a visit to his father's grave. That incident
was ultimately attributed to excitement and the shock of his
recent injury, but it gave everyone who was with him at the
Arlington Cemetery quite a scare—especially when Max's little sister Rory also fainted shortly after seeing her brother
pass out.

During a childhood visit to Sargent and Eunice Shriver's
house, Max got hit in the head by a descending staircase
elevator. He was knocked unconscious and ended up in the
intensive care ward in the hospital. Luckily, his injury was
not as serious as first suspected, and he was sent home shortly
after he woke up.

Max attended the Moses Brown School, graduating in
1983. This was about the time that he began what can be
described as a search for his father. Many of the younger
RFK kids—those children who have no or very little recollection of their dad—have attempted to better understand their
slain father by reading about him and his work and trying to
see beyond the icon. Their search is a personal quest to better
know their father—even though their ultimate knowledge of
him and his work can only be gleaned from secondhand

sources. In the July 1997 issue of *Life* magazine, Max revealed that he was compiling a book of his father's favorite quotations, "the words that inspired him," he said, "and the words he left to inspire us."

One of the less visible offspring of Ethel and RFK, Max graduated from Harvard in 1987 with a degree in American History, and ultimately earned a law degree and passed the bar. He worked for a time as a law clerk in the Philadelphia district attorney's office before becoming an assistant DA there. He has worked for the Citizens Energy Corporation (the company founded by brother Joe II and run by brother Michael) and has also been involved in Citizens Conservation. In the fall of 1997, Max entered business school at UCLA.

The subtitle of this chapter refers to a nickname given to Max by his Philly colleagues during his time there in the DA's office. In September 1992, Max saw a man attempting to break into a car. After shouting at the crook and ordering him to stop, Max personally chased him on foot for three blocks. The hapless crook ended up running right into the arms of a Philadelphia cop. After that incident, Max's celebrated Kennedy name took a back seat to his new moniker: Elliot Ness.

Max married Victoria (Vicki) Anne Strauss, also a lawyer, on July 13, 1991, and today they live in Los Angeles and have two children, Matthew Maxwell Taylor Jr. and Caroline Summer Rose.

Douglas Harriman Kennedy

(b. March 24, 1967)

THE RECORD BREAKER

I am often asked if I want to follow my father. I want to follow him, but I want to make my own tracks.
—DOUG KENNEDY's answer to a prep school application
question

Douglas Harriman Kennedy's birth made his mother a happy woman.

A new child always imbues its parents with great joy, but Douglas' arrival was a landmark event in the Kennedy family annals: Because he was RFK and Ethel's *tenth* child, Ethel officially broke mother-in-law Rose's record of nine children. There were now *two* supermoms named Kennedy, and it was *Ethel* Kennedy—not Rose—who was the winner in the Kennedy motherhood marathon. The world noticed this landmark event, and close to twenty-five photographers chronicled Douglas' journey from Georgetown University Hospital home to Hickory Hill.

Born six weeks early by Cesarean section, Douglas joined the Kennedy clan weighing in at five pounds, four ounces. He was born with hyaline membrane disease, a potentially deadly lung condition that seems to run in the Kennedy family. JFK and Jackie's son Patrick died shortly after birth from the condition, and John Kennedy Jr. was also born with it, but recovered completely with treatment, as did Douglas — even though Douglas was in extremely critical condition and near death in his early hours of life. Douglas' big brother Joe II was the first of his siblings to see Douglas during his twenty-day stay in the hospital after he was born. Ethel went home after a week.

Douglas was named after his two "honorary" godfathers, former Treasury Secretary Douglas Dillon, and Truman administration diplomat and former New York Governor W. Averell Harriman. After recovering from his lung condition and gaining seven and a half ounces in his first twenty days, Douglas was sent home, and was baptized on Father's Day, 1967, at St. Luke's Catholic Church. Following this scare, the mood among Kennedy kin and friends was celebratory: at the Hickory Hill reception, guests ate caviar and drank champagne.

Douglas was only a year old when his father was assassinated, and even though he did not have any actual memory of RFK, this landmark tragedy must have had a significant effect on the development of his personality. It is understandable, then, why Douglas was reportedly very prayerful in his teenage years and was described as sensitive by his family and friends.

Douglas spent time with his brother David before his drug overdose death, staying in the room across the hall from David in the Palm Beach motel where David died. David and Douglas visited their grandmother Rose the weekend prior to David's April 1984 death. Apparently, both boys had been upset by the condition of their grandmother during their visit to the Kennedy compound, and Douglas did not want to remain in Florida. Douglas left Palm Beach the Monday before David's overdose on Wednesday.

Douglas attended the Potomac School and ultimately graduated from Brown University in 1990. He has worked in the media for years, including handling varied duties at the *Santa Monica News* in California. After heading back east to attend the Kennedy-favorite University of Virginia School of Law, Douglas then took a job as a general assignment reporter for a weekly newspaper in Nantucket. He also worked for the *New York Post* for a time, but resigned in anger when the paper ran a story reporting that Doug's father RFK had had an affair with Jackie Kennedy. Other media jobs Doug has tackled have included heading the cable news operation TCI, and a job with the Fox News Channel as an on-air reporter.

In April 1997, Douglas subbed as an anchor on a Fox Network Sunday news broadcast shortly after the news had broken that Douglas' brother Michael was being investigated on alleged statutory rape charges for a rumored affair with a babysitter that began when the girl was only fourteen years old. The Michael Kennedy story was everywhere, and yet, there was no mention of the allegations in Douglas Kennedy's newscast. When queried about the omission, a Fox spokesman replied that they had skipped a Michael Kennedy story because "there was nothing new to report." A New York paper reporting on Douglas' broadcast titled the blurb, "Spin Cycle."

Today Douglas is still single and working for the Fox Network as a reporter and on-air anchor. Even though he is in a high-profile career and spends much of his time in front of the cameras, he rarely comments on Kennedy family matters, preferring to focus on news not involving his well-known name.

In an interview with *Life* magazine in July 1997, Doug was asked if he found it odd being a journalist in a family "hounded by the press." Doug replied, "Some of my father's best friends . . . were journalists. They were my heroes."

Rory Elizabeth Katherine Kennedy

(b. December 12, 1968)

THE TRAILBLAZER

Even if I have different politics than Eunice, and Eunice has different politics than Grandma, and even if I have different politics from my sister Kathleen, there is continued respect for people who have chartered the way. It's to the credit of the women in the family that attitudes have changed, and to a certain extent to the credit of the men as well, but it has definitely been a battle that has had to be fought, and continues to be fought.

— RORY KENNEDY

Rory Kennedy, now thirty, holds two distinctions among the Kennedy grandchildren. She is the youngest blood third-generation child born (Jean and Steve Smith's adopted daughter Kym Maria is younger), and she is the only child of Ethel and RFK born after RFK's assassination. Ethel Kennedy was three months pregnant with Rory when RFK was shot. Following her husband's funeral, Ethel tried to resume as normal a life as possible, even to the point of continuing to play tennis well into the latter months of her pregnancy. Ultimately, she ended up agreeing to stay in bed for her final few weeks after she almost miscarried Rory in October of 1968.

Some of the people around Ethel during this time speculated that she harbored ambivalent feelings about her unborn child due to the fact that she knew this would be the last child of Bobby Kennedy's she would ever bear. In fact, one of Ethel's nurses, Luella Hennessey, speaking in Jerry Oppenheimer's biography of Ethel Kennedy, *The Other Mrs. Kennedy*, described the mood in the delivery room during Rory's birth: "I thought it would be very upsetting for Ethel when the baby was born because it would never see its father. It was kind of a traumatic few minutes, but then everything was fine."

During Rory's delivery, Ethel stayed in the same private room in Georgetown University Hospital that she had occupied when she gave birth to her son Douglas. Unlike Doug, though, Rory was born healthy and large, weighing in at an impressive eight pounds, four ounces. Rory's uncle, Ted Kennedy, held Ethel's hand during the delivery, proudly standing in for his brother. Following Rory's birth, Ted Kennedy emotionally announced, "I now have sixteen children." He was, of course, referring to his brother Bobby's eleven, his brother Jack's two, and his own three.

Ethel chose the first name of Rory because she felt it was closest to "Bobby," and because she did not like the name Roberta. Her middle names, Elizabeth and Katherine, were for her friends Liz Stevens and Kay Evans.

Shortly after Rory's birth, Ethel Kennedy was named the Most Admired Woman in America in a Gallup Poll. The country obviously saw Ethel as heroic and strong, and held her in even higher regard than her mother-in-law Rose or her sister-in-law Jackie.

One week after Rory was born, Ethel and her new baby left the hospital. On the way back to Hickory Hill, Ethel made Rory's Uncle Ted take a detour: She instructed him to take her and the baby to Arlington National Cemetery. Once there, in a scene that had to have been terribly moving and poignant, Ethel "introduced" Bobby to his new daughter.

Rory is part of a new breed of Kennedy women. She is the first third-generation female to declare herself a feminist, vocally and passionately aligning herself with women's issues and rights when she was twenty-four. This is a remarkable personal stand, considering the fact that the Kennedy clan, if anything, is known for being a "boys' club," a patriarchal fellowship in which the men have usually made the rules and had all the fun.

From an early age, Rory was a champion of the Kennedy women. When her grandmother Rose was in her eighties, several of her grandchildren wrote and staged a production called *The Story of Rose*, a play which told the story of the Kennedy family matriarch's life. Rory appeared in the production: she played her grandmother Rose during what may have been the most important time of her life—her son Jack's presidential campaign and his election as president.

Rory majored in women's studies at Brown University, but has not limited herself to focusing solely on feminist issues. In December 1988, Rory and her brother Douglas were arrested outside the South African Embassy in Washington, DC for protesting against apartheid. Charges were later dropped. In December 1992, Rory was quoted in *Cosmopolitan* magazine talking about what she felt her obligations as a Kennedy were: "I think I have a responsibility to do whatever makes me happy," she said. "I don't feel I have to do something in the political realm if I don't want to." This philosophy has spawned an interesting career path, one closer to that of her cousin Chris Lawford the actor, than it is to her lieutenant governor sister Kathleen or her State Representative brother Joe.

Rory is an independent documentary filmmaker. She has

done research all over the country and around the world—
from Harlem to Namibia—and at one point she produced
videos in Washington, DC; shot films that looked at important
women's issues—including some that were volatile and contro-
versial, such as the criminalization of crack-addicted mothers.
The Kennedy Foundation has embraced her work and provided grants to help her continue making films.

Today, Rory is unmarried and lives in New York, where
she produces her independent documentaries. She keeps a
relatively low profile and apparently chooses to express her
passion for sociocultural improvement and progress through
her films. Recently, however, Rory did speak candidly about
the dominant perception of her family and the larger issue of
what she sees as an often sexist, male-dominated culture:

> It's not that the boys in my family were horrible, but
> an indicator of a larger social phenomenon. The battle
> isn't fought in our family simply over who sits at the
> head of the table at Thanksgiving. It's fought out in
> the world against institutions that limit women, that
> we demand that women are represented in a more
> empowering way, that women be allowed to be priests,
> that we have all our reproductive rights, that we get
> respect from medical doctors and hospitals. That's the
> struggle, not simply for the Kennedy women, but for
> all women.

As the youngest third-generation Kennedy feminist, Rory
may have more ideologically in common with her nieces than
with her sisters and her cousins. Perhaps in years to come,
Rory's nieces will also put on a production about one of the
strong Kennedy women, but with one important difference:
this time the production just might be called *The Story of Rory*
instead of *The Story of Rose*!

THE CHILDREN OF
JEAN KENNEDY AND
STEPHEN SMITH

Stephen Edward Smith Jr.

(b. June 28, 1957)

THE KENNEDY NAMED SMITH

Because our family is so close, the loss of Uncle Jack and Uncle Bobby was very much like losing our own parents. After Bobby died, especially. I had this powerful sense of the awful possibility that someone very close to me could be taken from my life. When you sense that, it can bring a sense of immediacy to what you do. You make the effort for others that you otherwise might not make, and you become very aware of trying to use your time the best way possible.

—STEVE SMITH JR.

Steve Smith Jr. is the eldest child of Jean Kennedy and Stephen Smith and the Smith son that no one ever hears about. He is, of course, the older brother of William Kennedy Smith, a man whom the world heard quite enough about a few years back. As a child, Steve Jr. enjoyed the zone of anonymity that came with having the last name of Smith. He was most certainly a Kennedy grandchild, but this wasn't obvious unless people knew who his mother was.

Steve attended St. David's School and the Collegiate School as an adolescent, and graduated in 1975. Steve was one of the lucky cousins who got to play with Caroline and John Jr. at the White House when JFK was alive. From there, he moved on to Harvard, graduating in 1979, and ultimately earned a law degree from the Columbia Law School. For a time, he taught international relations and political ethics at Harvard and is still, at fortysomething, a single guy, making him one of the more eligible Kennedy bachelors.

Throughout his life, Steve Jr. has drawn great inspiration from the lives of his two assassinated uncles. He has said that he has vivid memories of everything surrounding RFK's death and funeral, can quote from memory from some of his uncle Bobby's speeches, and he cites the death of JFK as the seminal moment when he realized that he was different from other people because of the family that he came from—and that he would be treated as such his entire life if people knew who he actually was.

As was common for many of the younger generation of Kennedys, Steve Jr. traveled the world when he was growing up, often for humanitarian or philanthropic causes. He worked with the Navahos one summer in his teens with his cousin Michael Kennedy; traveled to South Africa in 1977; and also worked in a refugee resettlement camp in Thailand in 1979, where he learned to speak Thai and lived on three hundred dollars a month.

In the summer of 1982, when he was twenty-five, Steve and his brother Willie traveled to Costa Rica, where they were warmly received when it was learned that he was a Kennedy. The Kennedys were much beloved at the time in Latin America. "It is impossible to describe the feeling you get hearing about how your family has made a difference to others," he told Kennedy biographers Harrison Rainie and John Quinn. "That trip brought it into focus."

Steve has not yet dived into the deep end of the political pool, although he has admitted that he has thought about being a "behind-the-scenes" boss like his father was when he was alive. Steve Sr., who died in 1990, was the "commander-in-chief" for the Kennedy dynasty. He handled business decisions for the clan, put out "crisis" fires through deft and savvy public relations skills, and was the troubleshooter and answer man for everyone in the family. Steve Jr. worked on his uncle Ted's 1980 campaign, and Kennedy watchers definitely consider him a potential political candidate at some point in his life.

Steve has said that it was almost a given that people in his family went into politics. So far, he has resisted the temptation. If Steve Jr. does get into politics, though, it will likely be with a "tough-as-nails" strategy and mindset. Insiders have always considered Steve to be the toughest of the twenty-nine Kennedy grandchildren. When he was young, he was a good amateur middleweight boxer. When Steve was boxing, one of his sparring partners was the legendary American writer Norman Mailer. The story is also told of the many times Steve's cousins would hold him down and "torture" him when he was a kid. He would never cry, no matter what they did to him. Instead, he would defiantly tell them "In your eye!" This earned him the childhood nickname of "Spitter."

Another tale told of Steve Jr. that is illustrative of Steve's toughness was an incident that occurred at Harvard. It seems that a bunch of "townies" started harassing Steve and his closest cousin, Michael Kennedy. Things got rough, and Steve ended up with a broken hand from defending himself and his cousin. The townies left them alone after that.

Today, Stephen Smith Jr. is involved in politics only tangentially: when he taught international relations at Harvard, he considered political issues in the abstract by evaluating the global situation and helping his students understand the worldwide political paradigm. He now works for the Conflict Management Group, teaching the art of negotiation, and working with everyone from African diplomats to Boston gang members.

Steve's father was an extremely influential figure in the Kennedy family. Steve Jr. may come to play a similar role in the family, but it may be as a low-profile adviser and manager, instead of in the limelight, or on the political trail. "I'm less inclined to be in an out-front role than some of the other people in my [extended] family," he told *Life* magazine in July 1997. "I'm perfectly satisfied to just do my own thing and have the esteem of the people I work with."

William Kennedy Smith

(b. September 4, 1960)

"FIRST DO NO HARM"

Any suggestion that I was involved in any offense was erroneous.
—WILLIAM KENNEDY SMITH's statement to the press after
being charged with sexual battery (rape) in Florida.

In 1981, William Kennedy Smith, then twenty-one, was present at an important Apache womanhood ceremony in Arizona in which his cousin Kara Kennedy participated as one of the ritual dancers. The undeniable irony of this particular young man witnessing a rite that exalted and honored women would not become apparent for an entire decade.

Here is the unavoidable fact that Dr. William Kennedy Smith will have to live with for the rest of his life: no matter what his accomplishments or what medical accolades he receives, no matter how many people he successfully treats as a doctor, and no matter where he decides to live or whom he ultimately marries, his December 1991 rape trial will be the invisible presence haunting him throughout his life and assuredly coloring the public's perception of him forever.

❋   ❋   ❋

William Kennedy Smith was born on the Sunday before Labor Day, September 4, 1960, the second child of Jean Kennedy and Stephen Smith. Even though William Kennedy (whom everyone in the Kennedy family has called "Willie" from an early age) was certainly a Kennedy, having the last name of "Smith" gave him and his siblings a zone of anonymity while growing up. Willie's early life, as befitting a Kennedy grandchild, was one of privilege, and yet it seems as though the Smiths were not the most "domestic" of families.

An extremely telling anecdote that reveals a great deal about how Willie was raised was recounted in Laurence Leamer's exhaustive biographical study, *The Kennedy Women*. This incident occurred at the Kennedy compound in Hyannis Port when Willie was nineteen and apparently quite inept domestically. He was staying at the house during a break from his studies at Duke, and one morning, he slept late and upon awakening and coming down to the kitchen, imperiously ordered the family's cook to make him breakfast.

When the cook refused, Willie began arguing with her, and the noise summoned his cousin Kerry, who intervened and demanded an explanation for all the yelling.

"This lazy bum comes in here," the cook angrily complained to Kerry, "it's ten o'clock, and he wants me to cook him breakfast." Kerry turned to Willie and suggested he make himself cereal and toast and not bother the cook. Willie agreed to fend for himself, but admitted to Kerry, "I don't know how to fix it." Kerry patiently explained how to make toast and then opened one of the kitchen cabinets and showed him several boxes of cereal. Willie was amazed at the gargantuan boxes of cereal: "I always thought," he explained to Kerry, "cereal only came in those little boxes like you know in the restaurants."

Willie and his brother Stephen were closest with John Jr. and Caroline (John and Willie are the same age), and often spent afternoons playing at the White House. Because they both had children in the same age group, Jean Kennedy and Jackie shared a maternal bond. Willie has maintained similar close ties with John into adulthood. It is possible that Jean also shared with Jackie the feeling that the RFK brood were, as a group, too boisterous and reckless, since neither mother allowed her young children to socialize with the Hickory Hill bunch all that much. Jean and Jackie also shared a passionate commitment to helping advance the Kennedy family's political goals: Jean was back on the campaign trail stumping for Jackie's husband, JFK, less than six weeks after little Willie was born.

When Willie was three, the Smiths lived on Fifth Avenue in New York City, and Jean could often be seen frolicking with him in Central Park on pleasant afternoons. In *The Other Mrs. Kennedy,* author Jerry Oppenheimer tells a funny story about the seven-year-old Willie, involving Kennedy family friend and noted writer Art Buchwald, and a pet chameleon. During one of his infrequent visits to Hickory Hill, Willie and his chameleon took second place in a pet show that was judged by Buchwald. Willie was terribly upset that his pet had not won first place, and when he complained to Buchwald, the good-natured writer played along, telling Willie there was a possibility that he had misjudged Willie's most noble of pets. Willie put the chameleon down on the ground, and when it began to skitter away, Buchwald exclaimed that he didn't know the lizard could walk and promised to send Willie a special blue ribbon when he returned home.

In his adolescent years, Willie attended St. David's School with cousin John and often spent time with John on Aristotle Onassis' island of Skorpios during the time Jackie and Onassis were married. As Willie grew into his teens and early twenties, his mother Jean personally introduced him to many of the movers and shakers in New York, exposing him to the worlds of high finance, literature, journalism, music, and the arts. Since he was a Kennedy, it was assumed that he would attend Harvard, as did many of his uncles and cousins. Willie opted instead for Duke University, and after graduating in January 1983, took some time off before enrolling at Georgetown University Medical School in 1987.

Like many of his cousins, Willie was afforded the opportunity to travel the world, and in the summer of 1982, he visited Costa Rica, where he was welcomed as a hero when the natives learned that his mother was one of the legendary Kennedys. After a period working for an investment banking firm in the early eighties (a period in which he learned that he definitely did not like working in the financial world), Willie traveled through China and its environs for over a year, from February 1984 through December 1985. He learned to speak passable Chinese and even spent some time working as a volunteer lab assistant at a Seventh Day Adventist hospital in Taiwan.

Willie is supposedly more reserved, more guarded, and more cautious of strangers than are some other members of his family, and yet there are disturbing reports of significant personality changes when he drinks. Barbara Gibson, Rose Kennedy's longtime personal secretary, writing in *The Kennedys: The Third Generation,* said that Willie was "shy when sober, [but] self-centered after drinking too much beer." Gibson also felt that Willie could be "potentially boorish in sex." This brings us, inevitably, to a discussion of William Kennedy Smith's December 1991 rape trial.

This regrettable event, now known as the Palm Beach scandal, embarrassed the Kennedy family and humiliated Willie. It also cast Senator Ted Kennedy as a pitiable bar-hopping boozehound, and it forced John Jr. to publicly degrade himself by showing up at the trial for no reason other than to be photographed with Willie in a blatantly manipulative ploy intended to exploit John's popularity as part of Willie's defense. Rumor has it that John's mother Jackie was told in no uncertain terms that if she did not persuade John to go to Palm Beach, the Kennedy family would not support John if he ever did decide to enter politics. The fact that John went to Palm Beach may be a clue as to John's intentions about eventually entering the political arena. The scandal also destroyed the reputation of a woman who only saw herself as a victim.

Did William Kennedy Smith rape Patricia Bowman on the grounds of the Kennedy family's Palm Beach estate on Good Friday evening, March 29, 1991? A jury made up of two men and four women deliberated just seventy-seven minutes before they returned with an acquittal for Willie, citing reasonable doubt that a rape had occurred. Yet Patricia Bowman was a very credible witness during the trial, and she further bolstered her believability by steadfastly refusing any and all offers of payment for her story, choosing, instead, to finally talk to Diane Sawyer on network television for no compensation whatsoever.

Here, then, are the sordid details of the events that occurred on Good Friday, 1991. Conflicting and contradictory stories will be presented for the reader to make up his or her own mind.

Easter weekend, 1991. Members of the Kennedy family gathered at the Kennedy compound in Palm Beach, Florida, to celebrate the holiday together. Present at the house were family matriarch Rose Kennedy, her son Senator Ted Kennedy, Ted's sister, Jean Kennedy Smith, Ted's son, Rhode Island congressman Patrick Kennedy, Jean's children, medical student William Kennedy Smith and his sister Amanda, and family friend and former FBI agent William Barry and his family.

At 11:30 on Good Friday evening, Ted Kennedy got out of bed after fitfully trying to sleep for an hour. He woke his nephew Willie and his son Patrick and invited them both to go out for a drink with him. They got dressed and accompanied Ted to Au Bar, a favorite Palm Beach meeting place.

There are several minor variations in the details of the

time line and the minutiae of that evening, but these facts are essentially irrelevant. What *is* known is that all these Kennedy men did, indeed, end up at the pricey club, and it is also known that Au Bar is where Willie met Patricia Bowman. We also know that Ivana Trump and a party of twenty were also at Au Bar that evening, but they played no role in the events involving Ted and Willie.

Ted, Willie, and Patrick eventually met three woman that evening who ended up playing the most important roles in the scandal and subsequent trial: Patricia Bowman, Anne Mercer, and Michele Cassone. Anne first sat and had a drink with Ted and Patrick, but after she called Patrick a bore and Ted chided her for insulting a congressman, Patrick left the table and went to the bar, where he met Michele Cassone. The two danced a bit, then Patrick invited her back to the Kennedy house. She accepted and followed Ted and Patrick back to the compound in her own car. Anne Mercer had left Au Bar with her boyfriend Chuck Desiderio when Cassone and Bowman headed to the Kennedy estate.

Meanwhile, Willie had met Patricia Bowman. They apparently liked each other and spent some time dancing and drinking together. When Willie decided he was ready to leave, he saw that his uncle and cousin had already left, and so he was driven home by Bowman. When they arrived at the house, they parked outside for a while, and Bowman admitted making out with Willie in the front seat of her car during this time. Willie then asked Bowman if she wanted to see the estate and she said she did. At this point, Patricia Bowman took off her pantyhose in the car before walking along the beach to the house.

While walking on the beach, Willie asked Bowman if she would like to go for a swim. She declined his offer, then reported that Willie stripped naked in front of her. She was uncomfortable with this apparent exhibitionistic display and turned away and began climbing the stairs from the beach that led to the house. When she reached the top stair, she says Willie grabbed her right leg from behind. She broke free from his grip and began running across the estate lawn. He then tackled her from behind, pushed her down onto the grass, pulled up her dress, pushed aside her panties, and had intercourse with her. Willie claimed that Bowman helped him take her panties off and that she unbuttoned his pants prior to their having sex. Bowman says that during the attack she screamed, but no one came out of the house, and that after Willie ejaculated inside her, she hysterically ran into the house and, from the kitchen phone, called her friend Anne Mercer.

The time was now between four and four-thirty in the morning. When Anne answered the phone, Bowman told her that she had been raped and that she needed her to come and pick her up at the Kennedy estate. After she hung up, Willie walked into the kitchen, and Bowman said to him, "Michael, you've raped me." Michael is the name of Patricia Bowman's wealthy stepfather, and the defense made a dramatic, completely unsubstantiated point of suggesting that Bowman had been raped by him and was projecting that trauma onto Willie. Bowman then claims that Willie told her that if she claimed he had raped her, "no one would believe her."

Shortly thereafter, Mercer and Desiderio arrived, and before they left the estate they took a photo in a plastic frame, a legal pad with a few phone numbers on it, and a decorative urn from the house. They testified that they took these items to prove to the police that they had actually been inside the Kennedy house. Bowman was taken home and did not report the rape that evening. She said she did not want to report it because she felt that no one would believe her word against members of a powerful family like the Kennedys.

The following morning, Holy Saturday, Bowman called a Rape Crisis Center around nine o'clock and the counselor there convinced her that she needed to go to the police and report the assault. She filed a formal report at two o'clock that afternoon, charging that she had been raped at the Kennedy home by William Kennedy Smith. She was taken to the hospital and an examination for sexual assault was conducted. She was bruised all over, and the doctors initially thought her seventh rib was fractured. (It turned out not to be.) They confirmed that full vaginal penetration had occurred recently and they recovered semen from her vaginal cavity. She told the police that Willie had not used a condom and, overall, Bowman was extremely distraught and on the verge of hysteria during the physical examination.

An official investigation thus began. It was learned that Bowman had had several glasses of wine and had taken the muscle relaxant Carisoprodol the evening of the alleged assault. The defense used this admission to design their case around the idea of Bowman having agreed to consensual sex while high on wine and pills and then regretting it after she sobered up. It was also suggested by Chuck Desiderio that Bowman had concocted the rape story to win favor with her wealthy stepfather, a businessman who had had an ongoing feud with the Kennedy family for years.

As soon as the police began the tedious process of interviews and evidence collection attempting to put together the case, the Kennedy public relations machine went into action. When detectives went to the Kennedy estate to question Ted and Willie, they were told that no one knew where they were, when actually the two men were in the house at the time. It was ultimately weeks before the police could talk to Willie or Ted and take blood and hair samples from Willie. It was also three weeks before Palm Beach police examined the Kennedy grounds for evidence, a period in which there had been rain and other weather that could easily have destroyed evidence.

After the charges against Willie became known, disparaging stories about Patricia Bowman began appearing in the press. Kennedy minions dug into Bowman's past and learned that she had had three abortions and had once been arrested for shoplifting. She also had many outstanding parking tickets, and all of these relatively innocuous revelations were used in a calculated attempt to discredit her and destroy her reputation before the case even got to trial. But Patricia Bowman willingly took a polygraph test and passed with flying colors. According to the results of the lie detector test, everything Bowman said about that night at the Kennedy estate was true.

After postponements from its August start date, the trial began on December 2, 1991. It was aired live on CNN, generating daytime audiences for the all-news station that were nine times as large as its usual viewership. Prosecutor Moira Lasch handled Bowman's side; attorney Roy Black defended Willie; Judge Mary Lupo presided.

Bowman's face was electronically covered with a blue dot during testimony in an attempt at masking her identity, but her name was already known throughout the world. The court presentation, including testimony by Willie and Ted Kennedy, lasted for ten days. The jury deliberated seventy-seven minutes and returned with an acquittal. Over five hundred people attended the trial, and during the proceedings, some wealthy Palm Beach estate owners were renting out their homes to the assembled press for up to $40,000.

Willie's mother Jean attended the trial almost daily, committing wholeheartedly to his defense. Her public statements were unequivocally supportive and reiterated the defense position that Willie was being framed: "I'm distressed that someone is trying to ruin his life and career when he's trying to help people," she told the press.

There were some very interesting elements to this trial, including the fact that Florida prosecutor Moira Lasch had attended the Stone Ridge Country Day School of the Sacred Heart—the same exclusive institution that Kennedy grandchildren Kathleen Kennedy and Maria Shriver had attended. Also, the defense's jury selection expert, Cathy Bennett, spent some of her last moments alive on earth helping Willie. At

the time of the trial she was dying of cancer, but she returned
to work because she truly believed that the sex had been
consensual and that Willie was being unjustly accused.

During the pretrial investigations, the prosecution found
at least three women who claimed that Willie had also attempted to rape them, including his cousin Max Kennedy's
girlfriend, who claimed Willie tried to rape her after a party.
"He was quite charming," Max's girlfriend told the Palm
Beach County State's Attorney's Office. "I felt completely
comfortable with him. I felt he was in no way trying to come
on to me."

Following a party, instead of staying at a friend's place as
she had planned, Max's girlfriend felt comfortable enough
with Willie to take him up on his offer to stay overnight in a
guest room at the Smith residence in New York. As soon as
they were in the guest room, Willie, according to what the
woman told the Palm Beach authorities, was all over her. "He
had his body completely covering mine and pinned me to the
bed. . . . He stayed on top of me . . . and he put his hands
on my breasts and up my dress," she said. "It was completely
unwelcome. I wanted it to stop immediately. I said, 'What are
you doing? Stop, Willie, get the hell off of me!' "

None of these women's testimony was allowed in court
although they, too, were extremely credible and did not look
for financial gain after telling their stories. None of these
women, however, said that Willie actually raped them. They
all said he came on to them aggressively and that they felt
threatened and were afraid they would not be able to rebuff
his advances. Again, this is where only the two people involved know precisely what went on. It is almost impossible
to ascertain from these types of conflicting stories precisely
when mutually consensual sexual foreplay crossed the line and
became attempted rape.

After his acquittal, Willie told the assembled media, "I
want to say thank you most of all to my mother. I don't think

it's possible for a child ever to repay the debt they owe their parents. I only hope I can be as good a parent to my children as my mother has been to me."

After the trial, Patricia Bowman faded into obscurity. She neither wrote a book nor did she make the rounds of TV talk shows. She lives a completely private life, perhaps still haunted by that infamous Good Friday, and likely still regretting her initially innocent meeting with one of the renowned Kennedy clan.

William Kennedy Smith continued his medical residency at an Albuquerque hospital, but cut it short in July 1993 after one year of a three-year program. There was an outbreak of the deadly Hanta virus at the hospital during this time, but Willie never said that that was why he left. There were reports that he told his family he was somewhat depressed during this time, and he ultimately moved to the Northwestern Rehabilitation Institute in Chicago to work with spinal cord injury patients and stroke patients.

Willie was back in the news in October 1993 when he got into a fight in a bar in Arlington, Virginia, after one of the patrons yelled out, "Hey, it's Willie the rapist!" Willie spent the night in jail and missed his cousin Joe Kennedy's wedding. He ended up receiving a sentence of one year's probation and a requirement to do one hundred hours of community service at a Chicago health clinic. The guy he punched filed a $500,000 civil suit which was settled out of court the day before the trial was scheduled to begin. After the settlement, Willie released a statement through his attorney, Gregory B. Craig, in which he said, "My friends and I were hassled, baited, and insulted by people who wanted to pick a fight with me. It was a difficult situation, and I wanted to defend myself. I regret what happened."

Today, William Kennedy Smith is an MD in Chicago, where he specializes in rehabilitative medicine. He has not been in the news since the 1993 incident. He is unmarried.

Amanda Mary Smith

(b. April 30, 1967)

GRANDPA JOE'S HISTORIAN

I was ever of opinion, that the honest man who married and brought up a large family, did more service than he who continued single and only talked of population.
—OLIVER GOLDSMITH, *The Vicar of Wakefield*

Amanda Smith, the *other* doctor in the Smith family, is one of the two adopted children of Jean Kennedy and Stephen Smith. Kym Maria, a Vietnamese orphan, is the other. Amanda has dark hair and a fresh-faced, all-American look that blends in naturally with the looks of her other Kennedy cousins.

Amanda's looks probably helped her mother Jean succeed in her oft-stated goal of making her two adopted children not feel like outsiders. According to published reports, it bothered Jean that Kym and Amanda were always referred to as the adopted Kennedy grandchildren. Jean and her husband Stephen, as well as Amanda and Kym's two brothers Willie and Steve Jr., made a conscious effort to assimilate these two young ladies into the Kennedy family as seamlessly as possible.

After they were adopted, the two girls were warmly received by the rest of the family. Kennedy family friend Andy Karsch told journalist Harrison Rainie that "[Amanda and Kym] are both really spectacular kids. They are the center of life in that house. They have great wit—true Smiths." In 1983, when Amanda was sixteen, her mother Jean repeatedly refused to discuss her adopted children with the media. "I don't want to talk about my daughters," she said. "I don't want them to feel different."

Reportedly, Amanda was shy as a child, but this is not uncommon with children who enter a new household due to an adoption. Nonetheless, her reserve did not change the way she was raised: she got the education and social training deserving of a Kennedy.

Amanda is close to, and strongly supports, her brothers and sister and was a visible daily presence at the Palm Beach rape trial of her brother Willie. Amanda and Kym would arrive at the courthouse early each morning and get in line for one of the precious courtroom seats available each day. But even though Amanda and Kym attended the trial, they reportedly sat in the back of the courtroom and visibly recoiled or cringed when they were inevitably approached by reporters or other courtroom observers, people almost salivating for some kind of comment from one of the Kennedys.

Amanda was artistic as a child and studied in France for a year. She ultimately went on to earn her PhD at Harvard in Special Education, and lives today, still single, in Boston, Massachusetts, where she is writing a book. This, in and of itself, is not unusual. There are a great many writers in the Kennedy family, and the younger generation was raised to respect literature, the arts, and the value of education. But when you consider that Amanda was *adopted* into the Kennedy family and then learn that she is writing a comprehensive biography of her grandfather, Joseph Kennedy, it becomes clear that this is quite an unusual development among the Kennedy grandchildren.

Of the twenty-seven surviving grandchildren, one of the two young women *not* of Kennedy bloodline was the one who decided to write about the patriarch of her family. This is a unique situation, considering that the only other books about the Kennedys written by family members have been written by cousins outside the inner sanctum of the immediate family.

What will Amanda Smith's editorial slant be? Will her book about her grandfather be a "warts-and-all" exposé— similar in tone to the recently published *Sins of the Father*—a tome certain to embarrass the family? Or will her book be a tribute to Joe Kennedy's ambition, perseverance, political achievements, and commitment to his family? The answers will be known when Amanda Smith's book is ultimately published.

In the meantime though, Amanda, now in her early thirties, lives quietly out of the mega-bright glare of the "Kennedy" spotlight and only surfaces when her family needs her, as in the case of brother Willie's troubles in Palm Beach. Her relative anonymity may vanish the day her book about Joe Kennedy hits the stands. How Amanda will be perceived by Kennedy watchers and her family will then be determined by what exactly this young PhD will have to say about the august head of her adopted family, the grandfather she never knew.

Kym Maria Smith

(b. November 29, 1972)

THE IRISH ONE

Freshly blows the wind to the homeland: my Irish child, where are you staying?
        —RICHARD WAGNER, *Tristan und Isolde*

Kym Maria Smith holds the distinction of being the youngest of all of the twenty-nine Kennedy grandchildren.

Kym was born in Vietnam in 1972 and was adopted by Jean Kennedy and Stephen Smith after the Vietnam War ended. In fact, Kym was one of the last of the many Vietnamese children air-lifted out of Vietnam as the United States abandoned the war and pulled out of the war-torn country. Kym was still a toddler when she was adopted by the Smiths, and thus probably has little or no recollection of her early life in Vietnam. She attended the Marymount School as an adolescent and then Brown University, graduating with her degree in the early nineties.

As a child, Kym was sociable and charming and reportedly could claim every single one of the Kennedy male cousins as admirers, ready and willing to do anything they could for her. Peter Emerson, a Kennedy family friend, once described Kym as "infectiously engaging." Completely lacking in pretense, when she was nine, Kym reportedly would insist that all visitors to the Smith home explain in detail what they did for a living and how they lived their lives.

When Kym was eighteen, she and her mother Jean spent some time together vacationing in Colorado. They then flew to Florida to spend the 1991 Easter weekend at the Kennedy family compound in Palm Beach. Kym was at the Palm Beach house when her brother Willie was alleged to have raped Patricia Bowman on the beach in front of the estate. Kym and her sister Amanda attended every session of brother Willie's trial, but refused to comment publicly on the charges against their big brother.

In 1995, Kym married Alfie Tucker, and for a time, they lived in Dublin, Ireland, on the ancestral land of the Kennedy clan. In 1997, Kym was reportedly living in New York, without her husband.

Kym Maria Smith Tucker does not appear in public with the Kennedys and keeps a determinedly low profile. She refused to be photographed for a 1997 *Life* magazine special issue about the twenty-eight Kennedy grandchildren. Nonetheless, she *was* raised a Kennedy (via the Smith branch) and ironically, even though she is probably the least likeliest Kennedy grandchild one would expect to return to the family's Emerald Isle roots, it can be said that of the twenty-eight Kennedy kids, Kym was one who could *truly* be dubbed *Irish*!

THE CHILDREN OF
JOAN BENNETT AND
EDWARD M. KENNEDY

Kara Anne Kennedy

(b. February 27, 1960)

TESTED BY TRAGEDY

*We studied the Cuban missile crisis, and it was hard to hear
the criticism that "President Kennedy used a macho style." You
want to be protective of the family. It's almost a sense of caring
too much and loving him too much that makes it hard to study
him now.*

—KARA KENNEDY

In *The Kennedy Women,* the story is told of the time Kara and
her mother Joan attended an April 1994 screening of the
acclaimed film adaptation of Isabel Allende's novel *The House
of the Spirits.* The movie starred Meryl Streep and Winona
Ryder, and Kara passionately empathized with these women's
troubles and admired their inner strength. After the movie
was over, Kara hugged her mother and told her, "That's what
we are, Mom, strong women."

Kara Kennedy Allen, Ted and Joan Kennedy's oldest
child and only daughter, today lives a happy and fulfilling
life. She's married to Michael Allen, a Washington, DC, architect, and is a stay-at-home mom with one child. Kara, who
resigned as media director of the Kennedy family's Very Spe-

cial Arts program when she decided to stay at home with her baby, keeps a low profile but supports the various Kennedy causes.

Her current happy life notwithstanding, though, it cannot be denied that Kara Kennedy had a somewhat traumatic and troubling early life; a life filled with tragedy and fear, a life that defined and transformed her.

Kara's early life certainly offered more than a young girl already burdened by a famous family and celebrated name should have had to deal with. She was one of those Kennedy grandchildren who tried not to divulge their last name to people when they were young. She once revealed that she had "strange people come up to me and try to kiss or hug me. After that, you learn to prize the ones who act normally."

JFK's assassination started these difficulties for her when Kara was only three. Kara was having lunch at the White House with her cousins the day of the assassination. Kara's father Ted's almost-fatal 1964 plane crash soon followed. A few years later, in 1968, her uncle Bobby was gunned down. Then, in 1969, when Kara was nine, her father drove his car into the water at Chappaquiddick and Mary Jo Kopechne tragically drowned. After Chappaquiddick, kids on the school playground would shout at Kara, "Your father killed a woman!"

A few years after that, Kara's brother, Ted Jr., was diagnosed with cancer and lost his leg. For a time, Kara feared she would "catch" cancer from her brother. Ted Kennedy's longtime aide Richard Burke also wrote in his revealing book, *The Senator*, that Kara was for a time jealous of all the attention Ted Jr. received because of his amputation surgery and followup care.

Now add to this maelstrom of tragedy her brother Patrick's lifelong battle with asthma and her mother Joan's ongoing problem with alcoholism, and it is easy to understand why Kara as an adolescent was extremely shy, overweight, and experimented with cocaine and pot. At one point, Kara's grandmother Rose wrote to her son Ted telling him to encourage Kara to speak out more. Rose, who felt Kara was much too emotionally closed off, also worried incessantly about Kara's weight when Kara was young.

Kara's mother Joan's alcoholism both traumatized and empowered Kara. When she was home, she would participate in "bottle searches," trying to find her mother's hidden stashes of alcohol. Kara attended Alcoholics Anonymous meetings with her mother. A friend of Kara's once remarked that of the immediate family, it was Kara who was her mother's primary support during her attempts at achieving sobriety.

Kara graduated from the National Cathedral School in Washington in 1978. She then attended Trinity College in Dublin, Ireland, for a time and was in Ireland when Ted Jr. had a bad chemotherapy reaction and had to be hospitalized. During Kara's second year at Trinity, her father insisted that she have two bodyguards with her at all times, after a deranged, knife-welding woman broke into Ted's Washington, DC, senatorial office.

Kara ultimately transferred to Tufts University, where she majored in public affairs. After college she took a job with Metromedia Television in New York City, and in 1988, she worked as the cochairperson of her father Ted's 1988 senatorial campaign. In 1990, she married Michael Allen in Our Lady of Victory Church in Hyannis Port. She briefly worked as a producer for WBZ-TV's *Evening Magazine* in Boston before leaving that position to serve as the media director of the Very Special Arts program in Washington, DC, a position she held for a few years until she resigned to stay at home with her and Michael's child.

Kara is especially close with her cousin Victoria Lawford and reportedly adores her cousin John Jr. She was one of those few Kennedy kin who attended one of John's performances in Brian Friel's play, *Winners*. Also, Kara and her brother Ted were the ones who threw John Jr. a going-away party before he left for his 1983 trip to India.

Today Kara is out of the limelight and it seems that's the way she likes it. Who can blame her for wanting to quietly enjoy her family after living through a stormy adolescence replete with death, illness, and emotional turmoil? Kara has never really expressed a personal interest in politics except to help out in other family members' campaigns. And yet she is, after all, a Kennedy, and the day may come when she decides to follow in her brother's and cousins' footsteps and run for elected office.

Edward "Teddy" Moore Kennedy Jr.

(b. September 26, 1961)

SMILING UNDERWATER

People hear so much and read so much they think they have an idea of what you do and who you are even before they've met you. They have a picture of you—mostly it's a media phenomenon—that is hard to shake. They see you the way they want to, not the way you are. I have often asked myself why this is so important to them, and I just don't know the answer.

I think I have to work twice as hard as others would because I'm a Kennedy . . . The pressure has gotten greater as I grew older. People expect you to make something important of your life. Kennedys really can't be on the sidelines.

—TED JR.

Ted Kennedy Jr. is the Kennedy grandchild who had cancer. That is how Kennedy watchers have always thought of Teddy, whom his family calls "TK," ever since he was twelve and the world watched him bravely totter out of Georgetown University Hospital on crutches after his right leg was amputated above the knee. His leg had to be removed to prevent the spread of a fast-growing cancer of the cartilage known as chrondosarcoma, and as things like this often do, this unfortunate event in Teddy's life has made him unique.

Teddy's cousin John Kennedy Jr., with whom he's close and shares some personality traits and characteristics, may hold the distinction of being the only member of the younger generation of Kennedys to have had books written about only him, but Teddy is the only third-generation Kennedy to have had a movie made about his life.

On November 24, 1986, in the middle of that year's November sweeps period, NBC aired a two-hour, made-for-TV movie called *The Teddy Kennedy Story*. This film dramatized the events in Teddy's life from before his cancer operation thirteen years earlier on November 17, 1973, through his summer trip to Ireland about a year later.

This 1974 trip to Ireland was the emotional center of the film's storyline, since it was during this trip that Ted Jr.'s father, Senator Ted Kennedy, realized that his son was not, in his own words, "a cripple." From his hotel window, Ted Sr. worriedly watched Teddy play goalie in an impromptu (and taboo) soccer game. After seeing his son make a great save during the game, the realization struck the senator that even though Teddy was missing his right leg, he was fully capable of doing almost anything and everything he set his mind to.

The Teddy Kennedy Story had an impressive $2 million budget and boasted an "A-list" creative team. The movie starred Hollywood veterans Craig T. Nelson (*All the Right Moves, Silkwood*, TV's *Coach*) as Senator Kennedy, and Susan Blakely (*The Towering Inferno, Rich Man, Poor Man*) as Teddy's mother Joan, and thirteen-year-old newcomer Kimber Shoop in his film debut as Teddy. The TV movie, which renowned film critic Leonard Maltin liked and rated "above average," was directed by Delbert Mann, who had previously won an Academy Award for his work helming the 1955 Ernest Borgnine classic, *Marty*. The script for *The Teddy Kennedy Story* was penned by Roger O. Hirson, the screenwriter who had earlier written the TV movie *The Last Days of Patton*, and who would again revisit Kennedy territory in 1991 with his screenplay for the three-part television miniseries, *A Woman Named Jackie*, based on C. David Heymann's book about Jacqueline Kennedy Onassis.

In a December 1, 1986 interview with *People* magazine, Teddy admitted that he resisted agreeing to participating in a movie based on his life for a long time. "A lot of things have been written about me and my family," he said, "and they don't come out the way they were supposed to. We're a very private family, and I was very cautious." He finally came to the realization that the movie was going to be made whether he gave his blessing to the project or not, and thus agreed to work with the production company, Entertainment Partners.

The film's coexecutive producer, Robert Fuisz, had first approached Teddy in 1982 when he was a senior at Wesleyan University. Teddy at first said yes to the film, but then changed his mind because he felt it would interfere with his last year at school. The fact that Fuisz and his colleagues delayed the film and respected Teddy's wishes—against the repeated urgings of lawyers and the network—convinced Teddy he could trust them. "We didn't want to be part of the multitude who have prospered at the expense of the Kennedys," Fuisz told *People*.

Ted Jr.'s fee for the film was almost $100,000, and it all went to Teddy's nonprofit group, Facing the Challenge, a Boston organization that works to help change policy toward the handicapped in corporations, academic institutions, and government agencies. "This film," Teddy told *People*, "could have an incredible impact." And so it did.

Teddy Kennedy Jr. was born on Tuesday, September 26, 1961, and was named Edward Moore Jr. after his father. He was Ted and Joan Kennedy's second child, and he grew up in a privileged, yet disciplined, atmosphere.

The Ted Kennedy household unapologetically had rules, and they were enforced. Ted's kids had chores to do for which they received an allowance. If they didn't do their chores, they didn't get their allowance. Also, if Teddy, Kara, or later, Patrick, broke or lost something, they were expected to pay the replacement cost for that item out of their admittedly small allowances.

Even though Ted Kennedy was a prestigious United States senator and came from a wealthy background and famous family, his children were not allowed to be rude or disrespectful to the household's domestic staff. Theresa Fitzpatrick, who was one of the children's governesses when they were growing up, has said that Ted's kids were instructed that she was not a maid, but instead, "she's someone who helps Mummy."

It was deeply ingrained in Ted's kids that they were not to consider themselves special simply because of their family. One of Ted's staff members remembered that Ted Jr. didn't learn that he was wealthy until he was fourteen and read a newspaper article which said he would inherit a fortune when he got older. Teddy had to ask someone what the word "inherit" meant.

As a toddler, Teddy played with many of his cousins and was having lunch at the White House on the day JFK was assassinated. As a child, Teddy attended St. Alban's School in Washington, DC. While there, he played football and was a good student.

Teddy was in the seventh grade at St. Alban's when his nanny discovered a protruding hard red lump about half the size of the boy's kneecap three or four inches below his right knee. Since Teddy was an extremely active and sportsminded young man, they were used to seeing all manner of bumps and bruises on his body, but this one seemed different—and within a couple of days, it had grown alarmingly larger.

After Senator Kennedy had been informed about the lump, he asked Dr. Philip Caper, a member of the senator's Subcommittee on Health, to examine Teddy's leg. Dr. Caper didn't like the looks of the lump and called in Dr. George Hyatt, the head of the Orthopedics Department at Georgetown University Hospital. Dr. Hyatt immediately called in a team of experts from the DuPont Clinic in Delaware and the Mayo Clinic in Minnesota to examine Teddy, and they all agreed that the suspicious lump should be biopsied as soon as possible.

The Kennedy cousins are, for the most part, an extremely close-knit bunch. As with all families, they have their disputes and family problems, but overall, the twenty-eight surviving grandchildren are a remarkably cohesive group. This strong bond was dramatically illustrated when the family learned that the lump on Teddy's leg needed to be biopsied. Amazingly, all twenty-eight of Teddy's cousins descended on Georgetown to be with him during his initial surgery.

Within a few days of the initial examination, Dr. Kent Johnson of the Armed Forces Institute of Pathology performed the biopsy on Teddy and examined the frozen section of the tissue taken from the growth on the twelve-year-old's leg. The results of the frozen section were devastating: it was confirmed that Teddy had a malignant cancer known as chrondosarcoma, and the decision was made that his leg needed to be amputated as soon as possible. The medical team wanted to break the news to Teddy as soon as they could, but Senator Kennedy overruled the doctors and informed them that he would be the one to give his son the bad news.

Teddy's lower right leg was amputated on Saturday, November 17, 1973, the same day that his cousin Kathleen was marrying David Townsend. This presented yet another problem for the Kennedy family: Teddy's father, Kathleen's Uncle

Teddy, was scheduled to give the bride away, thereby taking the place of his slain brother, an honor he could not turn down.

As detailed in the earlier chapter on Kathleen Kennedy Townsend, Ted Sr. stayed at Georgetown University Hospital with his mother Rose until he was given the word that Teddy's one-and-a-half-hour surgery had been successful and "uneventful" and he was assured that his son was doing fine. Interestingly, during the operation, Teddy's grandmother Rose Kennedy paced outside of Teddy's hospital room repeating over and over what can only be described as a "Kennedy mantra": "One must not be defeated. One must not be defeated." After being given the news, Ted Kennedy then rushed to the church, where he dutifully walked his niece Kathleen down the aisle. He then quickly returned to the hospital so he could be present when his son came out of the anesthesia.

During Teddy's surgery, immediately after the boy's diseased limb was removed, the surgical team fit him with a cast that slipped over the stump. This tight dressing was used to reduce swelling and facilitate healing.

The senator stayed at the hospital with his son every night for almost two weeks while his son was hospitalized. He went to the Senate for only two or three hours a day and arranged his schedule so he could eat every meal with Teddy, as well as be with him for all his physical therapy sessions. His family and friends had been frequent visitors to the hospital and the renowned artist Jamie Wyeth even did a painting of a farmhouse especially for Teddy. Determined and optimistic, Teddy walked out the front door of the hospital on crutches on Friday, November 30, 1973, to overwhelming media attention.

Eventually, in 1974, Teddy would wear an above-the-knee, semisuction prosthetic limb weighing seven and a half pounds and costing a thousand dollars. Teddy has been emphatically uninhibited about his prosthetic limb.

The story is told of the time Teddy was at a party and was wearing shorts that completely revealed his wooden leg. A woman at the party literally could not stop staring at his leg, and so Teddy handled the situation by taking a piece of cheese and cutting it into pieces on his leg. "See?" he said to the stunned gawker. "It makes a great chopping board!" Teddy has also admitted that one of the things that got him through the experience was the fact that his brother and sister did not treat him differently. Soon after he was walking on his artificial leg, Kara and Patrick were making bets on how far he'd get before falling on his face.

Even though Teddy's surgery was considered successful, his ordeal with cancer was far from over. In early 1974, doctors broke the news that Teddy should undergo twenty-four months of chemotherapy to be certain that the cancer had not spread anywhere else in his body. Teddy accepted this stoically, but has spoken frankly about his horrifying experience with the chemo regimen. Beginning in February 1974, Teddy and his father would travel to Children's Hospital in Boston every three weeks for three days of intensive chemotherapy treatments. The medical community had recently developed a new treatment for the type of cancer Teddy had. This treatment involved giving the patient enormous doses, two thousand times the usual therapeutic dosage, of a powerful and deadly chemotherapy drug called methotrexate, followed every few hours by a series of injections of an antidote to the toxic chemical, a drug called citrovorium.

Teddy would undergo six hours of painful injections as soon as he arrived at the hospital on Friday, and would then be violently ill for at least the next twenty-four hours. Ted Sr. learned how to give Teddy the antidote injections and would stay with him the whole time. Teddy has admitted that these treatments were so terrible and debilitating that there were times he actually wished he could die, and there were other times when he felt it would have been easier to just live

with the disease rather than endure the vomiting and unrelenting nausea. "But that's when my father and my friends were
so important," he has said. "They were always there, and that
presence was enough to get me through." Today, two decades
after Teddy's treatment, the debilitating side effects of chemotherapy are much more effectively managed and controlled. It
is not uncommon for people to receive intravenous bags of
chemotherapy drugs over an entire eight to ten hour period
and not report even a twinge of nausea.

During this almost two-year period, Teddy did not let his
treatments slow him down. In the summer of 1973, Teddy
went rafting on the Colorado River with his father and several
other family members and friends. In the spring of 1974,
Teddy and his family toured Russia. Later that summer of
1974, Teddy visited Ireland, and played soccer, an activity his
doctors probably would not have condoned. While visiting
Ireland that summer, Teddy had to be briefly hospitalized at
Saint Vincent's Hospital in Dublin because of side effects
from his chemotherapy treatments. In May of 1975, Teddy
toured the Mideast, including visits to Saudi Arabia, Iraq,
Iran, and Israel.

Even though Teddy was supposed to undergo twenty-four
months of chemotherapy treatments, it was determined after
eighteen months of the treatments that he was completely
cured and considered cancer-free and, thus, his visits to Boston stopped and he was able to live a relatively normal life.
And life went on.

During the summer of 1977, when Teddy was in his mid-
teens, he worked for $2.35 an hour directing cars on and off
the ferries that traveled from Cape Cod to Nantucket and
Martha's Vineyard. The following summer, Teddy had what
might be described as his most exotic summer job to date: at
the age of only sixteen, he worked as the recreation director
on a French cruise ship that stopped in several ports including
one in Egypt. While in port in Egypt, Teddy was the center

of attention: a group of children were fascinated with his artificial leg and pleaded with him to let them touch it. Teddy
good-naturedly complied.

During this summer, Teddy also took scuba diving lessons
and was so friendly and warm that his diving instructor remarked, "That boy even smiles underwater!" Teddy obviously
did not consider himself handicapped in any way, and because
he was athletic as a child—reveling in swimming, tennis,
camping, football, sailing, skiing, and other activities—as soon
as he felt up to it, he dove right back into his favorite sports.
He was even nominated in 1979 for a Valor in Sports Award.

Teddy traveled to Europe in 1979, where he met Pope
John Paul II, and in 1980, worked on his father's presidential
campaign. He and his aunt Jean Smith focused on issues
relating to the handicapped during the campaign.

Teddy enrolled at Wesleyan University after high school
and, like several of his cousins, got into a little trouble when
he was in his late teens and early twenties. In 1980, at the
age of nineteen, Teddy was arrested in New Jersey for possession of marijuana. In 1981, Teddy was stopped by the police on his way home from Wesleyan for speeding. While
stopped, police discovered marijuana, and Teddy ended up
paying thirty dollars in fines and court costs.

As an adult Teddy has kept a relatively low profile and
doesn't make headlines nearly as often as his more celebrated
cousins. He ultimately went on to major in ecology and receive a Master's Degree from the Yale University School of
Forestry and Environmental Studies.

In 1992, Teddy publicly revealed that he was an alcoholic,
and in June of that year, voluntarily checked himself into the
Institute for Living in Hartford, Connecticut, for a three-week
rehabilitation program. Of this unfortunate turn of events,
Teddy has said, "At times, life has presented me with some
difficult challenges, and I am doing my best to face up to
them. My decision to seek help was based on my belief that

continued use of alcohol is impairing my ability to achieve the goals I care about."

On October 10, 1993, Teddy married Katherine "Kiki" Gershman, a bright and personable woman who is now a psychiatrist in New Haven, Connecticut. There is an amusing story told about Teddy's earlier "love life": when he was younger, Teddy had so many girlfriends that his mother Joan would instruct photographers to always place Teddy's latest at the end of a line so that she could be more easily cropped out when Teddy "moved on," which he did on a regular basis.

Teddy enrolled in law school (which he completed attending nights) and also worked as the director of community projects for the lead-detection program of the Yale Medical School's pediatrics department. He holds the distinction of being responsible for overseeing the construction of the world's first completely lead-free house. Teddy is still involved with Facing the Challenge and other organizations dedicated to helping the handicapped and disabled, including the Special Olympics. He and Katherine have one child, Kiley Elizabeth, and live in New Haven, Connecticut, where he works for a large law firm. So far, he has not publicly expressed any political ambitions, although he is a vocal supporter of his brother, Rhode Island Congressman Patrick, and his equally politically-minded cousin Joe II, a representative from Massachusetts.

Teddy experienced great personal challenges above those inherent of being a Kennedy, and yet he came through it stronger and more confident of his capabilities. He has achieved great things in his life in the past twenty-five years, and he did it all with a smile on his face—even when paddling around underwater.

Patrick Joseph Kennedy

(b. July 14, 1967)

IN SHADOW NO MORE

There are groupies around all the time and I need my friends to tell me who is being genuine and who isn't. Sometimes you can't tell until it's too late.
— PATRICK KENNEDY

In the year 2004, John F. Kennedy Jr. will be forty-four years old, and there are some Kennedy watchers who speculate that he might challenge incumbent President Al Gore in a primary for the Democratic nomination for president. This assumes, of course, that Al Gore runs for president in the year 2000 at the conclusion of Bill Clinton's eight-year run as chief executive, and that he is elected. But even if John Jr. does not run, there is still the possibility that there *will* be a Kennedy on the ballot that year. Senator Ted Kennedy has publicly predicted that his son, Patrick Kennedy, currently a congressman from the state of Rhode Island, will run for president in 2004.

Even though the conventional wisdom has long been that John F. Kennedy Jr. is the Kennedy dynasty's last chance at the White House, there are a great many political theorists who see Patrick Kennedy as a viable candidate. There are also others who look to Joseph Kennedy II as an eventual Kennedy candidate for higher office.

If Patrick Kennedy does run for president in 2004, he will be only thirty-seven years old, one of the youngest presidential candidates in the history of the Union. And if he won, he would replace his uncle Jack as the youngest president ever elected.

Patrick Joseph Kennedy is the youngest of Ted and Joan Kennedy's three kids. As a little boy, he was described by one writer as "a cross between Peter Pan, a leprechaun, and Huck Finn." And true to his Emerald Isle heritage, when he was young, Patrick had a "thatch of strawberry blond hair, innocent emerald eyes, and freckles."

In his youth, Patrick had severe bronchial asthma and had to repeat the third grade because he missed so much school that year due to his illness. Patrick had to carry a portable Medihalor with him at all times, and Ted Kennedy learned how to give him his steroid injections. The senator was extremely diligent in making sure he gave his son the medication. When Patrick was young, he drew a cartoon of his father as an ogre wielding a terrifying hypodermic needle. This creation of Patrick's was titled "My Night Nurse."

Ted tried to spend a lot of time with Patrick when the boy was little. In his 1980 book *The Kennedy Children: Triumphs & Tragedies*, Bill Adler quoted the senator as remarking, "I spend as much time with him as I can. In the evening in winter we try to play as much outdoors as possible. He likes Frisbee, tennis, and soccer, and he's a very good card player—crazy eights—or we play backgammon or Ping-Pong."

Once, when Patrick was eight, renowned newspaper columnist, author, and Kennedy family friend Art Buchwald visited the Kennedy compound in Hyannis Port and decided to take some of the grandchildren on a little "field trip." Buchwald took a bunch of kids to visit a nudist beach on Martha's Vineyard. In retrospect, this is a funny story and something in character with the irrepressible Buchwald. But at the time, it wasn't so funny. Ethel Kennedy in particular was quite upset and is reported to have told Buchwald, "I'm never going to trust *you* with my children again!" But when Ethel asked eight-year-old Patrick about the trip and whether or not he had gawked at the naked people, the young boy replied, "No, I kept my hands over my eyes!"

Even though Ted and Joan were very concerned about Patrick's asthma and were both attentive to his medical needs, it seems as though they refused to coddle him in any manner at all, sometimes actually demanding much more of him when he was a child then he could reasonably handle.

In *The Kennedy Women*, Kennedy biographer Laurence Leamer tells the story of the time Patrick's grandmother Rose Kennedy came to visit her son Ted and his family. Rose was extremely displeased with what she perceived as the excessive demands being made on ten-year-old Patrick. The young boy came in the house to visit with his grandmother, and Rose was upset to see that he was "burning up." When she insisted on an explanation as to why Patrick was so overheated and obviously exhausted, the boy's governess explained to Joan that Patrick had done nothing but enjoy what she described as a "normal day." This "normal day," however, had actually consisted of "over six hours of exertion, obligations, and demands." Grandmother Rose was livid: "This is a little child," she scolded Joan. "Not an Olympic trainee!" And as only Rose Kennedy could do, she laid down the law to the chastened, and likely irked, Joan Kennedy. Patrick was to remain in bed for most of the following day, eating lightly and spending most of his time resting. Rose Kennedy was not going to stand by and watch her frail, asthmatic, ten-year-old grandson collapse from overexertion because his parents refused to let his asthmatic condition be an issue.

Patrick attended the Potomac School in Washington in his preteen years, before transferring to the Fessenden School in Boston in the early eighties. While attending the Fessenden School, Patrick won a football trophy for being the "most spirited" on the team. Patrick also wrestled at Fessenden in the 105-pound weight class. Like his cousin John, Patrick was one of the lucky ones who attended the elite Phillips Academy in Andover, Massachusetts, which he transferred to from Fessenden. After his mother and father separated and Joan Kennedy moved to Boston in 1978, Patrick decided to move to Boston in 1981 to be near his mother. He had initially stayed with his father and his brother and sister after Joan left.

Bill Adler wrote that as a child, Patrick was always his mother's "little shadow." He used to follow her around and would often plead with her to teach him to play the piano the way she did. Mother and son have had a very close lifelong bond, so it is understandable that, as close as Patrick was (and still is) to his father, he would prefer to live near his mother—especially when mother and father were ultimately living hundreds of miles apart. In 1982, when Patrick was fifteen, he and his mother took a trip to Israel, which Patrick later described as "the best time we have ever spent together."

Throughout his adolescent years, Patrick's family name preceded him and often caused problems. Even though Patrick was only two when his father drove off that infamous bridge at Chappaquiddick, the stench of the scandal lingered for years. Patrick was often tormented by classmates about the Chappaquiddick incident. "There were always little incidents aimed at me," he told Kennedy biographers Harrison Rainie and John Quinn in *Growing Up Kennedy*. "My father could always sense when things were wrong and he'd try to explain it to me."

Patrick helped his father during the senator's 1980 presidential campaign, traveling and stumping in 1979 when he was only twelve. He even took time off from school to be with his father during campaign stops. Once, during a stop in Nashville, Tennessee, Patrick was interviewed by reporters who wanted to know why he was out campaigning instead of in school. "I'm writing a journal about [the campaign] to take back to school," he told the assembled media. "I've written about three pages so far," he revealed. But being a Kennedy, when asked if he had any plans to eventually publish the journal, Patrick's thoughts quickly turned to the financial potential of his scribblings. "How much," he mused aloud, "could I sell it for?"

This campaign was not always easy for Patrick, however. Later, when asked about what it was like to be a twelve-year-old political campaigner, Patrick told one reporter, "That was tough. I was only twelve and I was very timid."

Like many of his other Kennedy cousins, in his younger years Patrick had problems with drugs. During his senior year at Andover, when he was nineteen, Patrick checked into Spofford Hall in New Hampshire, a drug rehabilitation facility, to beat a reported cocaine addiction.

"As a teenager, I had started down the wrong path in dealing with the pressures of growing up," he said in 1991. "I mistakenly believed that experimenting with drugs and alcohol would alleviate them," he told the Knight-Ridder News Service in response to a question about a *National Enquirer* story that spilled the beans on his Spofford sojourn. "I finally decided not to escape from those pressures, but to confront them."

Patrick moved to Rhode Island in 1986 and attended Providence College. He majored in philosophy, and apparently such contemplative study imbued in Patrick a passion for self-definition and helped him come to some important conclusions about what he wanted to do with his life. He ultimately earned his degree in social science. Patrick was quoted as saying that the study of philosophy clarified a need in him for "a sense of purpose and direction" in his life. Being a Kennedy, he found this purpose, of course, in politics.

Another factor contributing to Patrick's increasing fascination with politics was his experience working for his cousin Joe II on his 1986 congressional campaign. "That was really exciting," Patrick said after the election. "I realized it was time for the torch to pass to our generation." In July 1996, Patrick told journalist Michael Matza that he decided to enter politics "to find out how I fit into my family's legacy."

While at Providence College, Patrick embraced the "Kennedy calling" and set his sights on a political career of his own. Specifically, in his junior year, Patrick decided that he wanted to run for Rhode Island state representative. In typical Kennedy fashion, Patrick ultimately ended up spending $87,000 of campaign funds and his own money to win a part-time job that came with the enormous salary of $300 a year. Patrick beat John Skeffington, a five-year incumbent who simply could not compete with the "glamour" elements that were part and parcel of a Kennedy political campaign. Patrick's incredibly popular cousin John stumped for him, greeting voters with, "Hi, I'm John Kennedy. It would be great if you would vote for my cousin." During one campaign stop, Patrick's dad, Senator Ted Kennedy, arrived at a rally in a helicopter, a truly impressive display of political clout and Kennedy power.

Patrick served six years in the Rhode Island House of Representatives and was then elected to Congress in 1994. He was reelected in 1996 with seventy percent of the vote. The 1994 congressional race, in which Patrick ran against Kevin Vigilante, a thirty-nine-year-old doctor, was chronicled in a PBS documentary called *Taking On the Kennedys*. Patrick spent close to $1 million on this campaign and again enlisted the star power of his family. John Jr. showed up, shook hands, and signed autographs. Cousin Caroline also appeared, and Patrick did not hesitate to call on his father whenever he felt Ted's celebrity status would be helpful. Vigilante was roundly defeated and, as the narrator noted in the introduction to the PBS documentary, the good doctor received "the political education of a lifetime." Most political mavens believe that Patrick now has his sights set on the year 2000, when they are certain he will run for the Senate.

Patrick does not yet have the jaded, seen-it-all attitude so prevalent in many older politicians. Speaking of his first term as a congressman, he told the *Providence Journal,* "Like anyone else coming into a new experience, I was filled with a lot of anxiety about what was in store for me. I just concentrated on my job, keeping close to people I had a good sense had a good working-hand knowledge of how to be effective in the place."

During his brief career, Patrick has already made a name for himself and can boast of some notable accomplishments. A biographical profile available from his office lists the following achievements:

1. Preserved funding for senior nutrition and Meals on Wheels program by forcing a withdrawal of welfare reform proposal;
2. Fought successfully for Base Realignment and Closure Commission's recommendation to add 562 employees at Newport Naval Facility;
3 Developed a partnership between Brown University and NASA to study Narragansett Bay which will assist Rhode Island's business community.

Patrick has lunch with his father in Washington at least once a week without fail. He has said he greatly values these father-to-son, senator-to-congressman talks with Ted, and their similar careers have strengthened their already-close bond. "For me it's opened up, personally, a whole dynamic of our relationship that heretofore I haven't had the chance to have with him," Patrick told reporters in 1997. "So as a son for whom his father is the most important person in his life in a lot of respects, this is a big change for me"

Patrick is still single and has often been described as one of the most eligible Kennedy bachelors. However, he has a steady girlfriend who he has been seeing for over a year and has publicly said that she is "somebody I love tremendously." As for marriage, he says that, "I feel very comfortable with her but it hasn't gone to that stage yet." Tellingly, Patrick refuses to divulge his girlfriend's name to the press.

Patrick will undoubtedly be a major player in the political arena for many years to come. His legislative priorities include protecting Medicare and Medicaid funding, protecting Rhode Island's $900 million a year defense industry, working for legislation that would allow a tax deduction for college loan interest, and being a passionate advocate for gun control legislation. Recently, Patrick made news with his outspoken blast against the Republicans' effort to lift the 1994 ban on assault weapons.

"Shame on you, my God," he told the assembled lawmakers. "You'll never know what it's like because you don't have someone in your family killed. It's not just the person that's killed, it's the whole family that's affected."

Even though Patrick J. Kennedy still has the tousled good looks of the boy next door, what is most significant about his ongoing political career is that he is being taken seriously by politicos twice and, in some cases, men close to three times his age.

Patrick's last name may have helped initially get him elected, but it is his commitment to causes and issues that will get him reelected. Ultimately this commitment will determine whether or not Patrick Joseph Kennedy is *the* Kennedy who will someday reclaim the White House. As he told *Life* magazine in July 1997, "Having a last name like Kennedy enables

me to feel that I can get to certain people who will be able to find solutions, to change the status quo. So I'm using my name, but hopefully I'm using it in a way that it was meant to be used, trying to further the interests of those who don't have a voice."

Recommended for Further Reading

Adler, Bill. *The Kennedy Children: Triumphs & Tragedies*. New York: Franklin Watts, 1980.

Andersen, Christopher. *Madonna Unauthorized*. New York: Simon & Schuster, 1991.

Bishop, Jim. *A Day in the Life of President Kennedy*. New York: Viking, 1961.

Bly, Nellie. *The Kennedy Men*. New York: Kensington Books, 1996.

Cameron, Gail. *Rose: A Biography of Rose Fitzgerald Kennedy*. New York: Berkley, 1971.

Collier, Peter and David Horowitz. *The Kennedys: An American Drama*. New York: Warner Books, 1984.

David, Lester. *Jacqueline Kennedy Onassis: A Portrait of Her Private Years*. New York: Birch Lane Press, 1994.

DeGregorio, William A. *The Complete Book of U.S. Presidents*. New York: Barricade Books, 1993.

Gibson, Barbara. *The Kennedys: The Third Generation*. New York: Thunder's Mouth Press, 1993.

Heymann, C. David. *A Woman Named Jackie: An Intimate Biography of Jacqueline Kennedy Onassis*. New York: Lyle Stuart, 1989.

James, Ann. *The Kennedy Scandals & Tragedies*. Lincolnwood, IL: Publications International, 1991.

Kelley, Kitty. *His Way: The Unauthorized Biography of Frank Sinatra*. New York: Bantam Books, 1986.

Kennedy, Caroline and Ellen Alderman. *The Right to Privacy*. New York: Knopf, 1996.

Kennedy, John F., ed. *As We Remember Joe*. Hyannis Port, MA: privately published, 1944

Kennedy, Robert F. Jr. *Judge Frank M. Johnson, Jr.: A Biography*. New York: Putnam, 1978.

Kennedy, Rose Fitzgerald. *Times to Remember*. New York: Doubleday, 1995.

Kennedy, Sheila Rauch. *Shattered Faith: A Woman's Struggle to Stop the Catholic Church From Annulling Her Marriage*. New York: Pantheon Books, 1997.

Lawford, Patricia Seaman. *The Peter Lawford Story: Life with the Kennedys, Monroe and the Rat Pack*. New York: Carroll & Graf, 1988.

Leamer, Laurence. *The Kennedy Women: The Saga of an American Family*. New York: Ivy Books, 1994.

Leigh, Wendy. *Prince Charming: The John F. Kennedy Jr. Story*. New York: Signet, 1994.

Onassis, Jacqueline Kennedy. *The Uncommon Wit of Jacqueline Kennedy Onassis*. New York: Citadel Press, 1996.

Oppenheimer, Jerry. *The Other Mrs. Kennedy: Ethel Skakel Kennedy: An American Drama of Power, Privilege, and Politics*. New York: St. Martin's Press, 1994.

Rainie, Harrison and John Quinn. *Growing Up Kennedy: The Third Wave Comes of Age*. New York: Putnam, 1983.

Schlesinger, Arthur. *Robert F. Kennedy and His Times*. Boston: Houghton Mifflin, 1978.

Shaw, Maud. *White House Nannie: My Years with Caroline and John Kennedy, Jr.* New York: New American Library, 1966.

Sotheby's. *The Estate of Jacqueline Kennedy Onassis* (auction catalog). New York, 1996.

Spada, James. *Peter Lawford: The Man Who Kept the Secrets*. New York: Bantam Books, 1991.

Spignesi, Stephen. *The J.F.K. Jr. Scrapbook*. Secaucus, NJ: Citadel Press, 1997.

Stone, Oliver: *JFK: The Book of the Film*. New York: Applause Books, 1992.